Edward R. Murrow

and the Birth of
Broadcast Journalism

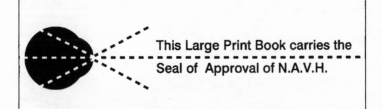

This Large Print Book carries the
Seal of Approval of N.A.V.H.

Edward R. Murrow

and the Birth of Broadcast Journalism

BOB EDWARDS

Thorndike Press • Waterville, Maine

Published in 2004 by arrangement with
John Wiley & Sons, Inc.

Thorndike Press® Large Print Biography.

The tree indicium is a trademark of Thorndike Press.

The text of this Large Print edition is unabridged.
Other aspects of the book may vary from the original edition.

Set in 16 pt. Plantin by Carleen Stearns.

Printed in the United States on permanent paper.

Library of Congress Cataloging-in-Publication Data

Edwards, Bob, 1947–
    Edward R. Murrow and the birth of broadcast journalism /
Bob Edwards.
       p. cm.
    Originally published: Hoboken, N.J. : Wiley, c2004,
in series: Turning points.
    Includes bibliographical references.
    ISBN 0-7862-6965-0 (lg. print : hc : alk. paper)
    1. Murrow, Edward R. 2. Journalists — United States —
Biography. 3. Large type books. I. Title.
PN4874.M89E38 2004b
070.92—dc22
[B]   2004056696

In memory of
Ed and Lois Bliss

As the Founder/CEO of NAVH, the only national health agency solely devoted to those who, although not totally blind, have an eye disease which could lead to serious visual impairment, I am pleased to recognize Thorndike Press★ as one of the leading publishers in the large print field.

Founded in 1954 in San Francisco to prepare large print textbooks for partially seeing children, NAVH became the pioneer and standard setting agency in the preparation of large type.

Today, those publishers who meet our standards carry the prestigious "Seal of Approval" indicating high quality large print. We are delighted that Thorndike Press is one of the publishers whose titles meet these standards. We are also pleased to recognize the significant contribution Thorndike Press is making in this important and growing field.

Lorraine H. Marchi, L.H.D.
Founder/CEO
NAVH

★ Thorndike Press encompasses the following imprints: Thorndike, Wheeler, Walker and Large Pr int Press.

Contents

Acknowledgments

I will be forever grateful to my editor, Hana Lane, for writing to ask if I'd like to be part of the Turning Points series of short books published by John Wiley & Sons. Hana let me pick my subject, giving me an excuse to write about the patron saint of my profession. With the focus strictly on Ed Murrow's innovations in radio and TV, large chunks of the man's life had to be omitted. For those who want to know more about Murrow, the Kendrick, Sperber, and Persico books listed in the bibliography will be most enlightening. I also recommend the Cloud/Olson book on the extraordinary group of reporters Murrow recruited for coverage of World War II.

Thanks to all at John Wiley & Sons who have had anything to do with this book.

Most of the material included here is drawn from thirty years of conversation with Edward Bliss Jr. Ed wrote for Murrow at CBS, then served as the first editor of *The CBS Evening News with Walter Cronkite*. After he retired from CBS, he founded the broadcast journalism program at American University in Washington, D.C. Ed's association with Murrow and Cronkite determined my choice of graduate school. I was Ed Bliss's graduate assistant for the 1971–1972 school year but remained his student for more than thirty years. My greatest regret is that when Hana asked me to write this book, I neglected to call Ed immediately and share my good news. Ed died two weeks later, at age ninety. His counsel would have been so valuable as I wrote, but he could not have told me anything he hadn't told me a dozen times over the previous thirty years. It would have been great just to share the moment with him.

Though a very sweet man, Ed was the toughest editor I've ever known, intolerant of imperfection. The second toughest is my very own wife. Sharon Edwards has a great eye for flawed construction, typing, grammar, and the like, but also for inflated rhetoric, hyperbole, and other nonsense from which her husband sometimes must be saved. She's made this a much better book than the one I first showed her. More important, Sharon has supported my career while raising three fabulous young people. Brean Campbell, Susannah Edwards, and

Eleanor Edwards provide their dad with the most rewarding conversations he has, even after a day of interviewing people making headlines.

Shannon Rhoades, Barry Gordemer, and Art Laurent of NPR were very helpful to me in writing this book. The enthusiasm of Andy Danyo for this project is enormously encouraging. Shelly Franklin Tillman makes my day job easier. Thanks to all of my colleagues at NPR for their daily collegiality in the nation's most interesting workplace. I am a lucky man to work with the best and the brightest.

Daniel Schorr, Bill Moyers, Richard C. Hottelet, and Casey Murrow were, after Sharon, the earliest readers of this work. Thanks to all of them for their comments and suggestions.

Casey Murrow is following his father's early path in a life devoted to education. In addition, Casey spends a lot of time on the legacy of his formidable parents and is the executor of their estate. I thank Casey for his blessing of this project.

Introduction

London, September 21, 1940. For weeks, the German Luftwaffe had been bombing Britain in preparation for a planned invasion. Initially, the targets had been military airfields, but in early September the strategy changed. Hitler struck London in the hope that the British people would beg their leaders to surrender. They bravely resisted instead. Describing Britain's finest hour to his American audience, CBS correspondent Edward R. Murrow made a different sort of history:

> I'm standing on a rooftop looking out over London. At the moment everything is quiet. For reasons of national as well as personal security, I'm unable to tell you the exact location from which I'm speaking. Off to my left, far away in the distance, I can see just that faint-red, angry snap of antiaircraft bursts against the steel-blue sky, but the guns are so far away that it's impossible to hear them from this location. About five

minutes ago the guns in the immediate vicinity were working. I can look across just at a building not far away and see something that looks like a flash of white paint down the side, and I know from daylight observation that about a quarter of that building has disappeared — hit by a bomb the other night. Streets fan out in all directions from here, and down on one street I can see a single red light and just faintly the outline of a sign standing in the middle of the street. And again I know what the sign says because I saw it this afternoon. It says, DANGER — UNEXPLODED BOMB. Off to my left still I can see just that red snap of the anti-aircraft fire. I was up here earlier this afternoon and looking out over these housetops, looking all the way to the dome of St. Paul's. I saw many flags flying from staffs. No one ordered these people to put out the flag. They simply feel like flying the Union Jack above their roof. No one told them to do it, and no flag up there was white. I can see one or two of them just stirring very faintly in the breeze now. You may be able to hear the sound of guns off in the distance very faintly, like someone kicking a tub. Now they're silent. Four searchlights reach up, disappear in the light of a three-quarter moon. I should say at the moment there are probably three aircraft in the general vicinity of London, as one can tell by the movement of the lights and the flash of the antiaircraft guns. But at the moment in the central area, everything is quiet. More searchlights spring up over on my right. I think probably in a minute we shall have the sound of guns in the immediate vicinity. The lights are swinging over in this general direction now. You'll hear two explosions. There they are! That was the explosion overhead, not the guns themselves. I should think in a few minutes there may be a bit of shrapnel around here. Coming in — moving a little closer all the while. The plane's still very high. Earlier this evening we could hear occasional . . . again those were explosions overhead. Earlier this evening we heard a number of bombs go sliding and slithering across to fall several blocks away. Just overhead now the burst of the anti-aircraft fire. Still the nearby guns are not working. The searchlights now are feeling almost directly overhead. Now you'll hear two bursts a little nearer in a moment. There they are! That hard, stony sound.

A live radio report of a war in progress was still rare in 1940. Listeners in comfortable living rooms all across the United States were hearing Britons being bombed in real time. Edward R. Murrow was adding another dimension to the field of broadcast journalism that he and William L. Shirer had launched just two and a half years earlier when Germany annexed Austria.

The two CBS correspondents had helped establish radio as a vital source of news and not just a place to hear game shows, dramas, and comedies. Radio as a popular entertainment medium was not yet twenty years old. Hearing Bing Crosby, Edgar Bergen, and Amos 'n' Andy might have provided momentary diversions from the burdens of the Great Depression, but World War II required that radio assume a new and important role.

Ed Murrow saw radio as a way to inform Americans about Nazi Germany's plans for Europe, a dark cloud Murrow spotted before most Americans who were not attached to government. To accomplish this, he assembled a team of smart and brave reporters whose accounts of the war would rival those of any newspaper staff and establish respectability for radio news. After the war, the expanded team carved out a spot for news in the new medium of television. Then, in 1954, Murrow demonstrated that TV news possessed a power beyond that of other forms of journalism. He and producer Fred Friendly focused the CBS eye on Senator Joseph McCarthy, exposing McCarthy as a despot and a bully.

The triumph of that accomplishment was short-lived, however, and in some ways marked the beginning of the end for Murrow at CBS. His exit from journalism seven years later is a story rivaling his spectacular entry. Murrow lost favor with his bosses, but never with his public. He left the scene with his integrity intact and a stunning record of accomplishment.

In just fifteen years, Murrow and company had introduced news to both radio and television — essentially creating broadcast journalism — to complement and compete with the more established media of newspapers and magazines. The initial stars of radio and TV had been vaudeville entertainers. Murrow, no less a star, gave broadcasting some class and a mission of public service beyond entertainment.

There was news on radio long before Murrow's first broadcast. Indeed, one of radio's most important early moments involved news — returns from the 1920 presidential election read over station KDKA in Pittsburgh. Radio was present for the marathon Democratic convention of 1924, the John Scopes "monkey trial" of 1925, and Charles Lindbergh's solo flight to Paris in 1927. Herbert Hoover's inauguration in 1929 drew a radio audience of sixty million. Firmly established as a force in American life, radio carried news of the kidnapping of Lindbergh's son in 1932. Three years later, millions listened to radio accounts of the circus trial of Bruno Richard Hauptmann, the man executed for the kidnapping and murder of the Lindbergh baby. Radio's first war correspondents covered Japan's conquest of Manchuria, Italy's invasion of Ethiopia, and the Spanish Civil War. The abdication of Britain's King Edward VIII was a huge radio event.

The most famous segment of audio from pre-Murrow radio news is an account of the *Hindenburg* disaster of 1937.

Herbert Morrison of WGN in Chicago went to Lakehurst, New Jersey, to record the landing of the German dirigible that had made eleven successful transatlantic crossings. This time, the ship burst into flames as it reached its mooring. Unprepared for such a gaseous explosion, Morrison sobbed his account into a microphone: "It's crashing! Oh, my! Get out of the way, please. And the folks . . . Oh, it's terrible! This is one of the worst catastrophes in the world. . . . Oh, the humanity! All the passengers! All the people screaming here."

The wags in today's newsrooms laugh when hearing "Oh, the humanity," but they weren't there that day and they didn't have to do Herbert Morrison's job. We should thank Morrison for having some humanity of his own as he watched thirty-six people lose their lives.

The coverage of news before Murrow came along was event-oriented. Stations and networks assigned staff to broadcast preplanned activities such as speeches, hearings, ship launchings, athletic events, and the like. Most didn't have professional reporters; they had announcers who might host a program of dance music one day and describe a boxing match the next.

To be a broadcaster in the early days of radio was to be a person who could handle any sort of assignment one might be given: a garden party, a circus parade, a religious revival, or a news conference. One wonders if today's broadcasting superstars could function as well as NBC's Graham MacNamee or CBS's Robert Trout in rotating daily among interviewing professors, hosting musical recitals, covering Ivy League rowing matches, and doing the talk-up to FDR's fireside chats.

Listeners also learned about world affairs through commentators, mostly famous newspaper reporters who had their own network programs. The best known were H. R. Baukhage, Elmer Davis, H. V. Kaltenborn, David Lawrence, Fulton Lewis Jr., Drew Pearson, Raymond Swing, Dorothy Thompson, Frederic William Wile, and Walter Winchell.

There was also a category of programming that radio called "talks," ranging from professors reading their scholarly papers to speeches and monologues by prominent figures in politics, business, labor, and science.

Such was the broadcast world Edward R. Murrow entered in 1935 as an arranger of chats and concerts to fill out the

CBS program schedule dominated by soap operas in daytime and celebrity entertainers at night. Three years later, Murrow, with Bill Shirer, would add another indispensable segment to the broadcast schedule — the nightly roundup of news from Europe, a continent then on a collision course with war. Murrow himself would host that program, and it would change broadcasting and journalism forever.

After the war, Murrow served briefly as a network executive, then resumed his radio broadcasts on a daily basis. Each summary of the news ended with a Murrow analysis that, from 1947 through 1959, addressed the Marshall Plan, the Berlin Airlift, NATO, McCarthyism, the Cold War, Korea, the polio epidemic, the Suez Crisis, the Soviet invasion of Hungary, integration in Little Rock, the launch of Sputnik, and the rise of Castro. In the middle of that remarkable radio run, Murrow, as coproducer and host of *See It Now*, also established television as a source of original journalism.

Murrow set the highest standard for the reporting of news on radio and television. His facts were solid, his scope thorough, his analysis on target, and his principles uncompromised. He was authoritative without being imperious. He engaged the high school dropout while not boring the intellectual. To this day he is cited as the example of how a broadcast journalist should function, although most people alive today never heard or saw him in a live broadcast.

Good looks and manners added to the Murrow legend. He was the classic tall, dark, and handsome man adored by women and envied by men. Impeccably dressed in tailored suits from London's Savile Row, Murrow had elegance balanced by a ruggedness he carried from his working-class boyhood. He was equally at ease with peasants and prime ministers.

He was not perfect, of course, but so many people thought him so that his flaws and mistakes were that much more shocking. He had dark moods that puzzled friends and coworkers. There were occasional exceptions to his high principles. He could be cold to friends, distant to family, and petty to rivals.

He was a chain smoker, as all his viewers could see, and he puffed his way through a 1954 program on the health hazards of smoking. His mother suffered from asthma and Murrow had bad lungs all his life, a life that ended in 1965 just two days after his fifty-seventh birthday.

Murrow's obituaries mentioned that he seemed a courtly prince who nevertheless championed the underdog, a sophisticated man with a common touch. *Variety* said he had brought television to maturity. He was hailed for his "unrelenting search for truth." The tributes pointed out that he had led CBS to greatness only to become expendable when his principles clashed with management. It fell to Murrow's biographers, however, to explore some of the deeper contradictions in his life, including the black moods and daylong silences that frequently haunted a man who had so many reasons to be happy. The man who oozed confidence on the air was a nervous wreck when about to begin a broadcast. The shot of whiskey he'd have to calm his nerves at airtime failed to stop his cold sweat or keep him from jiggling his leg in a continuous nervous tic.

America's foremost broadcast journalist put so much weight on his own shoulders that he could never be at peace. He was a driven man who demanded more of himself than he could possibly deliver. Murrow lived by a code too rigid for mere humans to meet. He expected more — of himself and others. Murrow's glass was always half empty. He felt the gloom of having his idealism shattered by reality.

1
Roots

Egbert Roscoe Murrow was born on April 24, 1908, at Polecat Creek in Guilford County, North Carolina. He was the last of Roscoe Murrow and Ethel Lamb Murrow's four sons. The firstborn, Roscoe Jr., lived only a few hours. Lacey was four years old and Dewey was two years old when their little brother Egbert was born.

There was plenty in Egbert's ancestry to shape the man who would champion the underdog. The Murrows were Quaker abolitionists in slaveholding North Carolina, Republicans in Democratic territory, and grain farmers in tobacco country. The Lambs owned slaves, and Egbert's grandfather was a Confederate captain who fought to keep them.

Roscoe, Ethel, and their three boys lived in a log cabin that had no electricity, no plumbing, and no heat except for a fireplace that doubled as the cooking area.

They had neither a car nor a telephone. Poor by some standards, the family didn't go hungry. Although the Murrows doubled their acreage, the farm was still small, and the corn and hay brought in just a few hundred dollars a year. Roscoe's heart was not in farming, however, and he longed to try his luck elsewhere. When Egbert was five, the family moved to the state of Washington, where Ethel's cousin lived, and where the federal government was still granting land to homesteaders.

They settled well north of Seattle, on Samish Bay in the Skagit County town of Blanchard, just thirty miles from the Canadian border. The family struggled until Roscoe found work on a railroad that served the sawmills and the logging camps. He loved the railroad and became a locomotive engineer. Roscoe was a square-shouldered six-footer who taught his boys the value of hard work and the skills for doing it well. He also taught them how to shoot.

Ethel was tiny, had a flair for the dramatic, and every night required each of the boys to read aloud a chapter of the Bible. The Murrow boys also inherited their mother's sometimes archaic, inverted phrases, such

26

as, "I'd not," "it pleasures me," and "this I believe."

The boys earned money working on nearby produce farms. Dewey and Lacey undoubtedly were the most profound influences on young Egbert. They likely would have taught him how to defend himself while also giving him reason to do so (although it's impossible to imagine any boy named Egbert not learning self-defense right away). It takes a younger brother to appreciate the influence of an older brother. If an older brother is vice president of his class, the younger brother must be president of his. If an older brother averages twelve points a game at basketball, the younger brother must average fifteen or more. The boy who sees his older brother dating a pretty girl vows to make the homecoming queen his very own. That's how it worked for Egbert, and he had *two* older brothers. He didn't overachieve; he simply did what younger brothers must do.

When not in one of his silent black moods, Egbert was loud and outspoken. For that reason, the kids called him Eber Blowhard, or just "Blow" for short. His parents called him Egg. In his late teens he started going by the name of Ed.

The boys attended high school in the

27

town of Edison, four miles south of Blanchard. Edison High had just fifty-five students and five faculty members when Ed Murrow was a freshman, but it accomplished quite a bit with limited resources. Ed was in the school orchestra, the glee club, sang solos in the school operettas, played baseball and basketball (Skagit County champs of 1925), drove the school bus, and was president of the student body in his senior year. English teacher Ruth Lawson was a mentor for Ed and convinced him to join three girls on the debating team. They were the best in their region, and Ed was their star. This appears to be the moment at which Edward R. Murrow was pulled into the great issues of the day ("Resolved, the United States should join the World Court"), and perhaps it's Ruth Lawson whom we modern broadcast journalists should thank for engaging our founder in world affairs.

The Murrows had to leave Blanchard in the summer of 1925 after the normally mild-mannered Roscoe silenced his abusive foreman by knocking him out. Fortunately, Roscoe found work a hundred miles west, at Beaver Camp, near the town of Forks on the Olympic Peninsula, about as far west as one could go in the then-forty-eight states. There was work for Ed, too.

After graduating from high school and having no money for college, Ed spent the next year working in the timber industry and saving his earnings. He was no stranger to the logging camps, for he had worked there every summer since he was fourteen. The camps were as much his school as Edison High, teaching him about hard and dangerous work. He also learned about labor's struggle with capital.

Throughout the time Ed was growing up, the Industrial Workers of the World (IWW), "the Wobblies," were organizing in the Pacific Northwest, pursuing their dream of "one big union." The powerful forces of industry and government were determined to snuff that dream. IWW organizers and members were jailed, beaten, lynched, and gunned down. A lumber strike during World War I was considered treason, and the IWW was labeled Bolshevik. Ed Murrow knew about red-baiting long before he took on Joe McCarthy. There was also background for a future broadcast in the deportations of the migrant workers the IWW was trying to organize. Near the end of his broadcasting career, Murrow's documentary "Harvest of Shame" was a powerful statement on conditions endured by migrant farm workers.

For the rest of his life, Ed Murrow recounted the stories and retold the jokes he'd heard from millhands and lumberjacks. He also sang their songs, especially after several rounds of refreshments with fellow journalists.

In the fall of 1926, Ed once again followed in his brothers' footsteps and enrolled at Washington State College in Pullman, in the far southeastern corner of the state. He earned money washing dishes at a sorority house and unloading freight at the railroad station. Halfway through his freshman year, he changed his major from business administration to speech. That's how he met one of the most important people in his life.

Ida Lou Anderson was only two years out of college, although she was twenty-six years old, her education having been interrupted for hospitalization. Childhood polio had left her deformed with double curvature of the spine, but she didn't let her handicap keep her from becoming the acting and public speaking star of Washington State College, joining the faculty immediately after graduation.

Ida Lou assigned prose and poetry to her students, then had them read the work aloud. She challenged students to express their feelings about the meaning of the words and whether the writer's ideas worked. Ed Murrow became her star pupil, and she recognized his potential immediately. She introduced him to the classics and tutored him privately for hours. Ida Lou had a serious crush on Ed, who escorted her to the college plays in which he starred. Years later, near the end of her life, Ida Lou critiqued Ed's wartime broadcasts. It was at her suggestion that Ed made that half-second pause after the first word of his signature opening phrase: "This — is London."

His fire for learning stoked and his confidence bolstered by Ida Lou, Ed conquered Washington State College as if it were no bigger than tiny Edison High. He was a leader of his fraternity, Kappa Sigma, played basketball, excelled as an actor and debater, served as ROTC cadet colonel, and was not only president of the student body but also head of the Pacific Student Presidents Association. He even managed to top all of that before he graduated.

In December 1929 Ed persuaded the college to send him to the annual convention of the National Student Federation of America (NSFA), being held at Stanford University in Palo Alto, California. At the convention, Ed delivered a speech urging college students to become more interested in national and world affairs and less concerned with "fraternities, football, and fun." The delegates (including future Supreme Court justice Lewis Powell) were so impressed with Ed that they elected him president. Ed returned to Pullman in glory. Often dismissed as a "cow college," Washington State was now home to the president of the largest student organization in the United States.

Ed's class of 1930 was trying to join the workforce in the first spring of the Great Depression. Banks were failing, plants were closing, and people stood in bread lines, but Ed Murrow was off to New York City to run the national office of the National Student Federation.

He was barely settled in New York before he made his first trip to Europe, attending a congress of the Confédération Internationale des Étudiants in Brussels. The conference accomplished nothing because divisions among the delegates mirrored the divisions of the countries or ethnic groups from which the delegates emerged. This was Europe between the world wars. The one matter on which most delegates could agree was to shun the delegates from Germany. Murrow argued that those young Germans should not be punished for their elders' actions in the Great War. The Europeans were not convinced, but once again Ed made a great impression, and the delegates wanted to make him their president. This time he refused.

Returning to New York, Ed became an able fundraiser (no small task in the Depression) and a master publicist, too. He convinced the *New York Times* to quote the federation's student polls, and he co-created and supplied guests for the *University of the Air* series on the two-year-old Columbia Broadcasting System. The arrangement with the young radio network was to the advantage of both organizations. Columbia enjoyed the prestige of having the great minds of the world delivering talks and filling out its program schedule.

The first NSFA convention with Ed as president was to be held in Atlanta at the end of 1930. Stunningly bold and years ahead of his time, Ed Murrow decided he would hold an integrated convention in the unofficial capital of deepest Dixie.

Howard University was the only traditional black college that belonged to the NSFA. Murrow successfully recruited half a dozen more black schools and urged them to send delegates to Atlanta.

Next, Murrow negotiated a contract with the Biltmore Hotel in Atlanta and attached to the contract a list of the member colleges. If the manager of the Biltmore failed to notice that the list included black colleges, well, that wasn't the fault of the NSFA or its president.

At a meeting of the federation's executive committee, Ed's plan faced opposition. Using techniques that decades later became standard procedure for diplomats and labor negotiators, Ed left committee members believing integration was their idea all along.

Then Ed made an appointment with Adolf Ochs, publisher of the *New York Times.* He told Ochs exactly what he intended to do and asked Ochs to assign a southern reporter to the convention. This later proved valuable when a Texas delegate threatened to disrupt the proceedings. The *Times* reporter, an Alabamian, asked the Texan if he wanted all this to end up in the Yankee newspaper for which he worked. The Texan backed off.

Housing the black delegates was not a problem, since all delegates stayed in local college dormitories, which were otherwise empty over the year-end break. The real test of Murrow's experiment was the closing banquet, because the Biltmore was not about to serve food to black people. Murrow solved this by having white delegates pass their plates to black delegates, an exercise that greatly amused the Biltmore serving staff, who, of course, were black.

Ed was reelected president by acclamation. Not for another thirty-four years would segregation of public facilities be outlawed.

2

Higher Ed

After another trip to Europe and the 1931 NSFA convention in Toledo, Ed was ready for a new challenge. He found it just a few blocks uptown from the federation's New York office. Dr. Stephen Duggan served as an adviser to the NSFA. Duggan was director of the Institute of International Education (IIE), part of the Carnegie Endowment. In 1932 Duggan hired Ed Murrow as his assistant.

This was Ed's introduction to the eastern establishment. Duggan had contacts with the elite of business, law, finance, government, philanthropy, and, of course, education. He was close to Franklin Roosevelt, who would be elected president that year. As Duggan's assistant, Ed was meeting everyone a future journalist needed to know. He also got to know their European counterparts. Educational exchange programs were the IIE's main business, and Duggan sent Ed to Europe in the summer of 1932 to evaluate scholars and others to be invited to lecture in the United States.

In December, Ed proposed to officials in the Soviet Union that summer courses in Moscow be available for American visitors. Similar programs had worked well in other countries, but the USSR was not like other countries. The program was begun, but Duggan and Murrow lost control of it. Just over two years later, the Hearst newspapers carried the story of a Communist propaganda school sponsored by the American IIE. In the 1950s Joseph McCarthy would use the Hearst story to smear his antagonist Ed Murrow.

Another part of Ed's new job was to attend educational conferences, including those of the organization he'd just left. On his way to the December 1932 NSFA convention in New Orleans, he stopped in North Carolina to visit relatives. A few days later, he reboarded the train in Greensboro and got to know the woman he would marry. Janet Brewster, a senior from Mount Holyoke College, also was on her way to the convention. They talked a great deal in New Orleans and exchanged letters after returning home. Ed found opportunities to conduct IIE business in places convenient for visits to the Mount Holyoke campus in South Hadley, Massachusetts.

Franklin Roosevelt was not the only election winner of 1932. Adolf Hitler was the new leader of Germany, and purges of German universities began shortly after the Nazis took control of government offices in Berlin in the spring of 1933. Twenty thousand books were burned in May, the same month in which the IIE responded to pleas for help. Stephen Duggan and the heads of twenty-one American colleges formed the Emergency Committee in Aid of Displaced German Scholars ("German" later became "Foreign"). Although officially its assistant director, Ed Murrow ran the emergency committee, and his work on its behalf over the next several years was nothing short of heroic.

The committee's goal was to find jobs for scholars no longer in favor in Germany. The project was sensitive for a variety of reasons. Germany was not yet at war with anyone and still enjoyed diplomatic relations with its European neighbors and with Washington. With the Depression under way, it was hard enough for American professors to find work; placing foreigners on American faculties took some explaining. It was understood that a number of those arriving from Germany would be Jews (although most were not). The committee also had to make certain that the scholars coming out of Germany were not potential propagandists for the Nazis, perhaps intent on stirring anti-Semitism on American campuses.

There was funding from the Rockefeller and Carnegie Foundations, which the committee supplemented through private donations. In effect, schools were being paid to accept world-class academics, including some Nobel Prize winners. Nevertheless, some of the country's elite universities, including Harvard, chose not to participate.

The German scholars became increasingly desperate, and there were more requests for help than the emergency committee could accommodate. The committee's efforts were making the Nazis look bad, and Berlin cracked down on one of the committee's affiliates.

Ed Murrow, meeting at all hours of the day and night with people seeking the committee's aid, finally took some time off and did something good for himself. He married Janet Brewster on October 27, 1934, at the Brewster family home in Connecticut. Ed took his bride to meet the relatives in Guilford County, North Carolina, then on to Beaver, Washington, for Janet's first meeting with her in-laws. They also went to Pullman to see Ed's mentor, Ida Lou Anderson, where Janet got a chilly reception. Ida Lou was still in love with Ed.

Janet knew that for Ed work came first, so when they sailed to Europe in June 1935 she had no illusions about a pleasure cruise. The meager funds of the emergency committee covered Ed's fare. To pay for Janet's fare, the two agreed to serve as social directors aboard ship. Janet, making her first trip to Europe, became seasick. Edward R. Murrow, future serious journalist, had to handle bingo night alone.

In London, committee work consumed him, and in Berlin he had secret meetings with strangers at all hours. He told Janet nothing, but she knew why.

The Emergency Committee in Aid of Displaced Foreign Scholars successfully relocated hundreds of Europe's greatest minds, including Paul Tillich, Martin Buber, Jacques Maritain, Thomas Mann, Herbert Marcuse, Felix Bloch, Kurt Lewin, Otto Nathan, and Hans Morgenthau. The benefits to American culture, education, science, the arts, and intellectual life would last for decades and well beyond if one considers that the scholars developed protégés whose students are still making contributions. Although Murrow preferred to focus on the thousands of applicants the committee could not help, years later he told an interviewer that his work with the committee was "the most satisfying thing I ever did in my life."

What can be said of a society that had no use for brains and chased them off to the United States? Hitler bragged that his Third Reich would last 1,000 years. He was exactly 987 years off the mark, and Ed Murrow would help document every nail in the Reich's coffin.

Americans who knew Murrow the broadcaster had no idea what he did for refugee scholars in the 1930s, the full extent of which would not be known until years after his death. On the other hand, Murrow in the 1930s did not know that he would become the quintessential broadcast journalist. He thought of himself as an educator, for everything he'd done since college had been connected to education. He imagined that someday he would be a college president. Even the next move he contemplated was related to education.

Ed was unhappy at the Institute of International Education. He valued Stephen Duggan as a mentor and father figure, but Duggan wasn't giving him much room to breathe. Although he was seventy years old, Duggan still wanted an assistant, not a successor. He was adamant about being in total control of policy. Ed was to handle governance, not policy. The IIE had become a dead end for Ed.

Arranging for Duggan to deliver a series of talks on network radio, Ed renewed the acquaintance of Fred Willis, who booked educational programs for CBS. The two had met in 1930 when Ed, still with the NSFA, sold Willis on the idea of the *University of the Air.* Willis wanted big names for the once-a-month broadcasts, and Ed brashly promised him Albert Einstein. Not only did Ed deliver Einstein, he followed with Mohandas Gandhi, German President Paul von Hindenburg, and British Prime Minister Ramsay MacDonald. Not bad for a college senior. Now it was five years later, and Willis wanted to focus on other duties at CBS. His educational programming responsibilities were being tucked into a new CBS post called director of talks, and he urged Ed to apply.

42

For all his accomplishments, Ed Murrow still lacked confidence. Born in a rustic cabin, the product of working-class parents, acculturated by lumberjacks, and educated at a "cow college" in the far West, Ed believed he needed to invent a bit more for himself. Applying to CBS, Ed added five years to his age, changed his college major to political science and international relations, and claimed to have an M.A. from Stanford. This was nothing new for Ed, although he had only inflated his age by two years when he went to work for the IIE. In 1934 Ed had been offered the presidency of Rockford College, then a women's school in Illinois. The deal fell through when the good ladies of Rockford discovered Ed was only twenty-six years old and didn't have the credentials they thought he'd had. Now, in September 1935, he was lying again to get a job at CBS, where he would establish a reputation for integrity and become a champion of truth.

The man to see at CBS was Ed Klauber, the deputy to the big boss himself, William S. Paley. A native of Louisville, Kentucky, and a former editor at the *New York Times*, Ed Klauber was Bill Paley's hatchet man, the ogre who struck fear into the CBS staff so Paley could remain the good guy above the fray. Klauber belittled underlings in front of everyone. He was so offensive that even Paley's attorney urged that Klauber be fired, but Klauber was too valuable. Employees expecting a pink slip trembled when summoned to Klauber's office.

Murrow was not intimidated by Klauber. Perhaps Murrow, twenty-seven, sized up the older man, forty-eight, and concluded that he'd seen tougher fellows in the lumber camps. Maybe Murrow enjoyed the security of having the option to continue his work at the IIE if the interview with Klauber didn't work out. What seems to have happened is that Murrow talked with Klauber and the two of them genuinely liked each other. Much later, Klauber, who didn't have a lot of friends in the world, asked Ed if he'd speak at his funeral. Ultimately, Ed fulfilled that commitment.

Klauber told Ed that the job did not involve going on the air. Ed was simply to arrange broadcasts by others. That was fine to Ed, who still saw his main direction in life as education. Journalism still was not in the picture, although his new post as director of talks included responsibilities previously handled by the director of news,

Paul White, and White resented it.

Paul White was a gruff-speaking, harddrinking practical joker described by Ed's assistant, Helen Sioussat, as a man who had seen the 1931 movie *The Front Page* too many times. Although White enjoyed showing his rough exterior to the world, he was no buffoon. Extremely well-read, he had been a star debater at Columbia University. A former wire service reporter for United Press, he was a good journalist, too. When UP and the Associated Press cut off service to CBS at the request of their newspaper clients, White hired hundreds of reporters across the country and created a viable news staff, forcing the wire services to surrender and restore their feeds to CBS.

White instantly recognized Ed as a rival, and not just because their turf sometimes overlapped. White wanted what Ed Klauber had, a corporate vice presidency in Bill Paley's inner circle. The polished, debonair director of talks looked like the sort of fellow Paley might prefer to White. The newsman tried to make others believe he was glad to be rid of the responsibilities that Murrow now assumed. He needled Ed about his good looks, dismissed him as a pretty boy, and played practical jokes on him. Sometimes their rivalry became juvenile, as in a shooting match to see who could hit more metal ducks at an arcade in Times Square, or in a drinking contest, which Murrow won.

White acknowledged that Ed had great contacts that paid off for everyone involved in programming at CBS during the busy news year of 1936. The network covered Hitler's increasingly repressive regime in Germany, the U.S. political conventions and election campaigns, Mussolini's war against Ethiopia, the abdication of King Edward VIII, and the New Deal programs for the Depression. Ed arranged for talks on these subjects in addition to presenting speeches by Leon Trotsky, John Maynard Keynes, and George Bernard Shaw.

Ed's work often involved political controversy, such as his decision to carry Earl Browder's acceptance speech as the nominee of the Communist Party. Having former president Hoover as the Republicans' "equal time" spokesman did not endear Ed to the Roosevelt White House. Ed's plan to present speakers on both sides of the Ethiopia question fell flat when the BBC decided that having a spokesman for Italy be heard in the United States through the BBC's circuit to New

York would violate League of Nations sanctions against the Fascist government in Rome. This was a lesson in the importance of a network controlling its own resources.

Ed did well in his learning year, and when Cesar Saerchinger, the CBS European director, decided he wanted to return home, Ed was chosen to succeed him in London. At first Ed was reluctant to go, wondering if he was being sent away as the loser in a power struggle with Paul White. Had colleagues not convinced Ed otherwise, a great career in broadcast journalism might never have begun.

Actually, Murrow's debut as a newscaster had already occurred. Emboldened by drink following the 1936 office Christmas party, Ed prevailed on Robert Trout to let him do Trout's evening newscast. Trout knew this was wrong, but Ed outranked him. Ed's performance was flawless, and no one in the company said a word about it to either of them.

Before leaving New York, Ed went to see James Seward, assistant treasurer at CBS. Seward suggested that he open a savings account for Ed and buy an insurance policy. In filling out the policy forms, Ed finally came clean about his age, telling Seward that the birth date listed in CBS personnel files was a "mistake." Seward and Murrow forged a bond of mutual trust, and for the rest of Ed's career, his finances were handled by James Seward.

With the move to London, Ed finally resigned as assistant director of the Emergency Committee in Aid of Displaced Foreign Scholars. He had been doing double duty for a year and a half, apparently without CBS knowing about it.

Ed and Janet sailed for England on April 1, 1937, just weeks before Ed's twenty-ninth birthday. He would be famous in time for his thirtieth.

3

Anschluss

Sailing to England with the Murrows aboard the SS *Manhattan* was the English political activist Harold Laski, whom they had met through Ed's work with the emergency committee. After a day of shipboard Ping-Pong, Ed told Laski that he didn't much care for England, particularly its class system, and that he wanted CBS broadcasts from England to be "down to earth." Laski, a Socialist advising the Labour Party, probably had even less use for the class system. He invited the Murrows to his summer cottage in Little Barfield, a village in Essex, and home of the Spread Eagle pub. Laski maintained that the English public house, where his lordship's son could be seen playing darts with the gardener, was Britain's last democratic institution. That was exactly what Ed wanted, and his broadcast from the Spread Eagle included the darts games and the robust singing of British and

American songs right up to the call "Time, gentlemen, please."

American broadcasts from Europe had little to do with the weighty issues of the day. Ed was in London to send home broadcasts of Wimbledon and the British Open, holiday celebrations from the Continent, flower shows, and maybe an occasional interview with a political figure. Radio was about entertainment, not news. Ed's predecessor in the job, Cesar Saerchinger, had broadcast the song of a nightingale from Kent, a feat that won praise from American radio editors as "the most interesting broadcast" of 1932. Ed continued to supply New York with as many features as he could arrange, sometimes displaying his "down to earth" bias, as in stories of a Cockney cab driver/philosopher.

The main job of the CBS representative in Europe was the same as the job of any CBS employee back home: beat NBC. William Paley's CBS was younger than David Sarnoff's NBC, which had two networks, the Red and the Blue, yet CBS had fought its way to becoming a worthy competitor for NBC. In Europe, CBS had far more catching up to do. Despite Saerchinger's coup with the nightingale, NBC was the American network with influence.

NBC's man in London was Fred Bate, who'd been living in Europe for twenty-five years and already had five years experience as Saerchinger's rival. NBC also had someone on the Continent, Max Jordan, a German-born former Washington correspondent. Bate and Jordan emphasized that they worked for the *National* Broadcasting Company, leaving Europeans with the impression that NBC was to America what the BBC was to Britain.

At least Ed had a great secretary, Kay Campbell, a young Scot fluent in French and German who would work with him for the next twenty-three years. Kay was shocked by the brazenness of her new boss when he asked her to phone Winston Churchill at the House of Commons or, if necessary, at his home. The way of doing business with important people in England was to write a formal letter and request an appointment. Kay got another shock when the right honorable member from Epping took the call. Churchill hoped an American audience, if not Parliament, might pay attention to his warnings of the Nazi military buildup.

Germany's rearmament in violation of the Treaty of Versailles was hard to ignore, although Britain and much of the rest of

Europe were doing their best. Memories of the Great War just twenty years earlier were too fresh. Students at Oxford (including American Rhodes scholar Howard K. Smith) had vowed to "not fight for king or country." Prime Minister Neville Chamberlain's policy was appeasement. Britain and France would not stand up to Fascism in Germany, Italy, or Spain. Adolf Hitler's government in Berlin saw pacifism as weakness and used the opportunity to build a mighty military machine.

Ed could see what was coming, and if he was going to report a war, he'd need some help to match the competition of NBC's Fred Bate and Max Jordan. Untrained as a journalist, Ed needed someone with a strong background in news.

The telegram from Ed Murrow requesting a meeting arrived at the perfect moment for William L. Shirer, who was walking the streets of Berlin to let off steam. Shirer had just lost his job with the Universal wire service, the overseas arm of Hearst's International News Service. Shirer was broke, living in Hitler's capital, and his wife, Tess, was pregnant. Murrow was promising nothing more than dinner but, given his situation, a free meal sounded good.

To get far away from his native Iowa and its values was Shirer's mission in life, and he'd done a good job of it. Graduating from Coe College in 1925, he earned passage to Europe by feeding cattle aboard the freighter that took him there. He had two hundred dollars that he blew on wine and women in Paris while looking for a job. On his last night before he had to return to Iowa, he was hired by the *Paris Tribune*. Two years later, he became a correspondent for the *Chicago Tribune* in Vienna, where he met and married Tess. Despite his important work on assignments in India and Afghanistan, Shirer's job was eliminated in 1932, a casualty of the Depression. Bill and Tess took the next year off in Spain, spending the thousand dollars they'd saved. Just as the money ran out, Bill got an offer from the *Paris Herald*. But Berlin was the Continent's most interesting place in the mid-1930s, and Bill Shirer went there in August 1934 as a reporter for Universal. The reporting he did from Berlin for the next five-and-a-half years formed the definitive account of Nazi Germany's march to war and was the basis for two of the best-selling nonfiction books of all time. But in the summer of 1937, Shirer, despite being one of the finest American correspondents in Europe, was a man in need of a job.

Shirer was everything Murrow was not. Shirer was a short, stout, rumpled-looking guy with thinning hair. He wore thick glasses, which he needed only for his good eye; he'd lost one in a skiing accident. He looked nerdy. Only late in life did Shirer appear charismatic, because he'd let the hair on the back and sides of his head (all he had) grow long. He looked like a foxy old folk singer who'd bedded coeds from Cambridge to Berkeley. In 1937, however, he resembled an accountant. How then to explain his fabulous success with women? He said it was because he tried so much harder than other men.

Murrow and Shirer's dinner date at Berlin's Hotel Adlon on August 27, 1937, began with Shirer taking one look at Murrow and concluding that he was the typical radio pretty boy of no substance. Once dinner was over and it was time for drinks at the bar, Shirer had concluded that his earlier assessment was completely wrong. For his part, Murrow found that Shirer was everything he'd been told about — sharp, knowledgeable, and well connected. Murrow offered him a job on the spot. There was, however, the matter of the voice test, strictly routine. New York hated Shirer's voice, Paul White being the biggest critic. That was all Murrow needed to hear. He hired Bill Shirer as Columbia's man on the Continent of Europe, based in Vienna, Tess Shirer's birthplace, and it was to be their baby's birthplace, too.

In his book *The Nightmare Years, 1930–1940*, Shirer wrote:

Murrow had fired me with a feeling that we might go places in this newfangled radio-broadcasting business. We would have to feel our way. We might find a new dimension for reporting the news. Instantaneous transmission of news from the reporter to the listener, in his living room, of the event itself, so that the listener could follow it just as it happened . . . was utterly new. There was no time lag, no editing or rewriting as in a newspaper. A listener got straight from a reporter, and instantly, what was taking place. The sound of a riot in Paris, of the Pope bestowing an Easter blessing in Rome, or of Hitler and Mussolini haranguing their storm troopers might tell you more than all the written descriptions a newspaper reporter could devise. Going over to radio, I thought, was going to be challenging and exciting.

The excitement came later. Shirer learned that New York's idea of his job was far different from his own. CBS regarded its European representatives, Murrow and Shirer, as impresarios arranging entertainments for an audience of curious Americans. Shirer was not hired to do what he best knew how to do. His *Berlin Diary* entry for October 7, 1938:

> Murrow will be a grand guy to work with. One disappointing thing about the job, though: Murrow and I are not supposed to do any talking on the radio ourselves. New York wants us to hire newspaper correspondents for that. We just arrange broadcasts. Since I know as much about Europe as most newspaper correspondents, and a bit more than the younger ones, who lack languages and background, I don't get the point.

It was Columbia that wasn't getting the point. All of Europe realized that Hitler's rearmament and the militarization of German society meant the Nazis were going to war. Austria was the obvious first trophy

Hitler would want (he'd said so in the opening lines of *Mein Kampf*), and CBS had one of Europe's best reporters stationed right there. As Shirer was arranging entertainment for oblivious Americans, he absorbed the increasingly ominous developments in Vienna.

The Nazis had staged an uprising in Austria in 1934. They killed Chancellor Engelbert Dollfuss, but their coup failed. The new chancellor, Kurt von Schuschnigg, jailed the Nazi leaders and outlawed the party. Now, four years later, Hitler was settling this score. On February 13, 1938, Hitler summoned Schuschnigg to Berchtesgaden and threatened to invade Austria unless Schuschnigg legalized the Nazi Party, released the Nazi prisoners, and installed some of them in the Austrian cabinet. Schuschnigg agreed, knowing he'd just signed off to the end of an independent Austria.

Shirer and Murrow tried to get the story on the air, but CBS in New York was not interested. Instead, CBS wanted its European operatives to arrange a series of broadcasts of children's choirs. Shirer went to Bulgaria on February 22 to broadcast a choir, spent his thirty-forth birthday aboard the *Orient Express*, and was met at the platform in Vienna on the twenty-sixth by an old friend who told him he was now a father. With great difficulty, Tess had delivered a baby girl. On the third day of labor, doctors finally resorted to a cesarean section. Afterward, Tess developed phlebitis.

On March 9, Schuschnigg made a desperate effort to save his country. He announced that there would be a vote on the thirteenth and Austrians would decide if they wanted to remain free from Germany. Shirer missed the announcement because he was on his way to Slovenia for another broadcast of a children's choir. Murrow was on a similar mission to Warsaw; children sang there, too. Returning to Vienna on Friday the eleventh, Shirer was in a cab on the way to the hospital to see Tess and the baby. Overhead, a plane dropped leaflets regarding the plebiscite, the first Shirer had heard of it. Tess was no better, and doctors feared damage from a blood clot. While Shirer was visiting Tess at the hospital, the situation in the streets was deteriorating. There were Nazi mobs out in response to the sudden cancellation of the plebiscite on orders from Hitler.

Arriving home, Shirer tried but failed to

reach Murrow in Poland to appeal for a CBS broadcast on the situation in Austria. Shirer then heard Schuschnigg on the radio saying he was capitulating to German demands that he surrender the chancellery to the country's top Nazi. Austria was done.

Shirer had the story to himself. NBC's Max Jordan was not in town. Shirer went to the studios of Austria's broadcasting network, hoping to get a shortwave broadcast to New York by way of Geneva or London, even Berlin, if necessary, although he'd have to contend with Nazi censors. Nazis now occupied the broadcasting building and told him no lines were available. He dashed over to Ballhausplatz in time to see the local Nazi leader declare a new National Socialist government. At a café, Shirer got a sense of the tragedy taking place. Political figures now out of favor made plans for escape or suicide. Jews, if they could, fled for their lives. Old friends betrayed one another. Shirer went back to the broadcasting offices to try again. This time Nazis turned him away at bayonet point.

Frustrated, Shirer went home and had a couple of beers. Hours passed, and he still couldn't get his big story on the air. Finally, Murrow called from Warsaw.

Hearing the news, Murrow suggested that Shirer travel to London and report his eyewitness account from there, free of censorship. Murrow would go to Vienna and cover the story in Shirer's absence. After phoning the hospital to leave a message for Tess, Shirer went to the airport.

A British Airways flight to London was overbooked with Jews fleeing the Nazis. Shirer offered lots of money for a ticket but understood why he had no takers. He succeeded in getting a flight to Berlin, then a Dutch flight to London, writing his script while aboard. At 11:30 P.M. (6:30 P.M. in New York) on March 12, 1938, William L. Shirer delivered his first report as a broadcast journalist, describing for Americans how Nazi Germany had carried out the *Anschluss,* the annexation of Austria.

For all his efforts, Shirer was beaten on the story. While Shirer was traveling to London, Max Jordan of NBC had hustled back to Vienna and persuaded the Nazis to let him broadcast. His account was censored, and he had not been an eyewitness, as Shirer had been, but he was first.

Back in New York, William Paley was furious that NBC was beating CBS, and he wanted his network to respond in dramatic fashion. In his autobiography written decades later, Paley said it was his idea to do a half-hour roundup, a single broadcast from multiple points in Europe. Only a couple of such broadcasts had ever been tried, and each took months of planning. The state of radio technology in 1938 involved having microphones in place, leasing shortwave transmitter sites and telephone long lines, arranging frequencies, and hoping that atmospheric conditions allowed the signal to be heard. Officials might need to be bribed and censors satisfied. Paley said he didn't want a delay, he wanted it that night — Sunday, March 13 — and he told Ed Klauber to make it happen.

Klauber had Paul White call Shirer in London to say New York wanted a roundup featuring Shirer and a member of Parliament from London; Murrow from Vienna; and American newspaper correspondents from Paris, Berlin, and Rome. White asked, "Can you and Murrow do it?" Shirer said yes and hung up, not having any idea how such a thing could be done.

Meanwhile, Murrow was having as much trouble getting into Vienna as Shirer had had getting out. Murrow ended up spending more than a thousand dollars of Paley's money to lease a twenty-seven-seat Lufthansa airliner and fly to Austria as its sole passenger. On the phone to Shirer, Murrow explained the technical arrangements needed for the roundup. Murrow's London secretary, Kay Campbell, undoubtedly gave Shirer much-needed assistance.

New York's call to Shirer was made at lunchtime, the cocktail hour in London. The roundup was scheduled for 8:00 P.M., New York time, 1:00 A.M. in London. Work that might have required days or weeks had to be accomplished in six hours — on a Sunday. The broadcast directors and chief engineers whom Murrow, Shirer, and Campbell had to contact would be difficult to reach. Negotiations had to be conducted in four languages among five European capitals hundreds of miles apart.

They recruited Edgar Ansel Mowrer of the *Chicago Daily News* to broadcast from Paris through special lines arranged because Paris didn't have a transmitter. Frank Gervasi and Pierre Huss of the International News Service were persuaded to speak from Rome and Berlin, respectively. Like other members of Parliament, Labor's Ellen Wilkinson was enjoying a weekend in the country until she was asked to quickly return to join Shirer at the BBC. In Vienna, the Nazis had reopened the circuit to New York, allowing Murrow to make his official broadcast debut.

At the appointed hour in New York, Robert Trout announced that the program *St. Louis Blues* would not be heard so that Columbia could present a special broadcast from Europe. Shirer began, saying Britain would protest Germany's action but not go to war. Then MP Wilkinson tweaked Tory appeasement, saying Britons (and their government) would merely be annoyed by Hitler's bad manners. From Paris, Edgar Mowrer said the world would now know that Hitler was a menace who stood for "brutal, naked force," but he added that France would not stand up to Hitler even though it knew what a German invasion felt like. Murrow was next from Vienna, saying, "Herr Hitler has not yet arrived." Then Murrow noted that Austrians fully knew their fate and how to respond: "They lift the right arm a little higher here than in Berlin and the 'Heil Hitler' is said a little more loudly." The program's only glitch was Gervasi's inability to persuade Roman radio officials to arrange a circuit out of the country on a Sunday. Shirer read Gervasi's script, dictated by telephone from Rome, saying Mussolini would not oppose Nazi actions in Vienna, as he had been prepared to do four years earlier. There were closing remarks from Washington by Senator Lewis Schwellenbach of the Foreign Relations Committee, who said German annexation of Austria was Europe's business. At 8:30 P.M. Eastern time the broadcast was over.

CBS in New York was thrilled and immediately ordered another roundup for the following evening (which turned out to include Murrow's account of Hitler's triumphant arrival in Vienna). "No problem," replied an exhausted but happy Shirer, who remained in London for more roundups that week. Murrow, Shirer, and company had just devised and executed what became the routine format for the presentation of news. It not only had multiple points of origin, it also had included both reporting and analysis of breaking news, and was both a journalistic and a technological breakthrough for broadcasting. No longer would radio news consist of announcers assigned to cover carefully preplanned events as if they were parades or mere curiosities. From this point on, network staff journalists would provide timely reporting and analysis of important breaking news.

Half an hour of radio news from Europe

did not compare to the depth of coverage still available in the major newspapers of the day, but radio could carry events in real time and analyze them shortly after. Radio also could reach millions of people in rural America and in small towns where newspapers carried little or no foreign news.

Another great discovery of the roundup, of course, was the emergence of broadcast journalism's patron saint and first great star. The onetime champion debater and speech major was a radio natural. Murrow was personable, smart, knowledgeable, authoritative, and pleasing to the ear. His career in education had been hijacked by journalism.

Ed visited Tess Shirer in the hospital every day until her husband returned from London. When Shirer did return, it was impossible for the pair of them to celebrate their broadcast journalism triumph, the birth of Eileen Inga Shirer, or even Tess's recovery, since she was still in critical condition and would require more surgery. The only celebrants in Vienna were Nazis, who'd begun the pattern of killing, looting, and terror they would sustain in every conquered capital for the next seven years. From Shirer's apartment, Ed and Bill watched Nazis loot the Rothschild mansion next door. Shirer took Murrow to a bar for a drink, but Murrow asked him to choose a different place. Ed had been to Shirer's bar on an earlier night and had seen a Jewish man take out a razor and slash his own throat. In India and elsewhere, the veteran Shirer had seen the horrors of war. Murrow was seeing such things for the first time.

4
The Blitz

As Shirer had predicted in that first roundup, Czechoslovakia would be Hitler's next target. Three-and-a-half million German-speakers lived in Czechoslovakia's Sudetenland. Hitler asserted that they were an oppressed minority and demanded that the Sudetenland be "returned" to Germany (which had never held it).

Britain's prime minister, Neville Chamberlain, had a plan. Off the record, he told Ed Murrow and other journalists that Britain, France, and Italy would cede the Sudetenland to Germany to make Hitler happy and preserve peace in Europe. Incredibly, Czechoslovakia was not to be a party to the deal and neither was the Soviet Union, which warned Berlin not to move on the Sudetenland.

Three times in September 1938 Chamberlain met with Hitler regarding the Sudeten Czechs. The third and decisive meeting was in Munich. German-born Max Jordan of NBC was given a copy of the final agreement, but it was Ed Murrow, monitoring Munich radio, who first announced to the United States that a treaty was signed.

Neville Chamberlain carried that piece of paper back from Munich to a hero's welcome in London. Hailed as Europe's savior, Chamberlain was cheered by crowds in the streets. There was talk of knighthood and perhaps the Nobel Peace Prize. Sober heads reasoned otherwise. Murrow and Shirer figured Hitler's next move would be made a year later, in Poland.

Both CBS and NBC made heavy investments of time and money in coverage of the Munich crisis, providing bulletins and specials around the clock. The CBS star this time was neither Murrow nor Shirer but commentator Hans von Kaltenborn, who would go by the less German-sounding H. V. Kaltenborn once the war began. Kaltenborn was a bit pompous but had a solid news background. During the Munich coverage, he slept on a cot in the CBS New York studio and did eighty-five broadcasts in eighteen days. As the *Anschluss* had spawned the roundup, Munich introduced the "roundtable," in which correspondents in different cities held a conversation rather than take turns reading scripts. Though NBC's Jordan and Fred Bate could still embarrass CBS, it was Columbia's team that was receiving the praise of critics on the strength of its on-air personalities. CBS and NBC spent $200,000 each covering Munich, an enormous sum then, and a measure of how far broadcast journalism had come in such a short time. Still, many Americans didn't understand what all the fuss was about. They wondered what this European problem had to do with them.

Events in Europe grew uglier in 1939. On March 15, German troops marched into Prague, and Spanish Fascists took control of Madrid two weeks later. Britain and France did nothing in either case.

Paley, Klauber, and White all supported Murrow's ambitions to expand the CBS reporting team in Europe in time for the outbreak of the war they knew was coming. Murrow continued the hiring pattern he'd begun with Shirer, recruiting people for their brains and not the sound of their voices.

Thomas Grandin was chosen for Paris. Grandin had no experience in broadcasting or journalism, but he was a scholar out of Yale and the Rockefeller Foundation and he knew all about France. The fact that Paul White hated Grandin's voice made him the perfect Murrow hire.

Eric Sevareid was next aboard. Sevareid and his wife, Lois, had called on the Murrows in London back in 1937 when the Sevareids first arrived in Europe. Murrow gave Sevareid his first look at television, which was already available in England. "There's the future," Murrow told him. The Sevareids went to Paris, and Eric's work with the *Paris Herald* and United Press attracted Murrow's attention. Eric, too, had the golden credential of having Paul White hate his voice.

White continued his rivalry with Murrow, who had become his subordinate when Murrow took the job in Europe. White enjoyed giving Murrow an order for a broadcast, then canceling the order, then changing his mind again when it was too late for Murrow to deliver the broadcast on the original date. This was designed to make Murrow look like a failure, but Ed was careful to save the cables in case he needed to document for New York what was really going on.

Hitler ranted on about Poland through the summer of 1939, but at CBS in New York, memories of Vienna and Munich seemed to have faded into the sweet isolation most Americans enjoyed. Americans wanted to hear about a Europe far different from Europe as it was. White ordered the CBS team in Europe to hit the nightspots of London, Paris, and Hamburg for a program called "Europe Dances." The idea that Europe on the brink of disintegration might be dancing was so repugnant to the Murrow team that they risked their jobs rather than produce the program. If they could have anticipated *The Producers*, a Mel Brooks musical decades in the future, they might have told White, "Goose step's a new step this year." Europe did not dance on CBS.

On September 1, Germany invaded Poland. Most correspondents in London predicted that the Chamberlain government would cave in to the Nazis once more, but not Ed Murrow, who said Britain would stand with Poland. Even Ed wasn't certain. Handing his script to British censor Cecilia Reeves, he asked, "Am I right on this? I have to be right!" He was right; appeasement was over. Britain and France declared war on Germany, and World War II was under way.

A week later, Murrow's competition made a huge mistake. NBC and the Mutual Broadcasting System suspended their coverage of news from Europe. Broadcasting was more rigidly regulated in 1939, and the networks were intimidated by warnings from the Roosevelt administration that the networks should behave responsibly during war. By the time NBC and MBS returned to war coverage a few months later, CBS had taken advantage and asserted itself as the leader in radio news.

Early in 1940, Ed's problematic lungs let him down. In Paris, he developed a case of pneumonia so bad that doctors feared for his life, but Ed insisted on returning to London as soon as his fever broke. He would have these periodic episodes throughout his life.

Shirer was back in Berlin now after a period based in Geneva. Grandin and Sevareid were in Paris. It was time for Ed to expand his team. Mary Marvin Breckinridge, a Vassar graduate, was an old friend from Murrow's days with the National Student Federation. She had also been aboard the ship that carried the Murrows to London. Previously a photojournalist, she became the first female full-time CBS news correspondent. She was based in Amsterdam, but circulated widely throughout Europe.

Larry LeSueur also joined the staff. After leaving NYU, LeSueur worked for United Press while moonlighting as a writer for CBS radio programs in New York. When UP wouldn't send him to Europe, he went on his own and looked up Murrow in London.

Cecil Brown, an Ohio State man, did newspaper work and put in time at two wire services before Murrow hired him to cover Italy. A former merchant mariner, Brown loved adventure on the water. His biggest was another year in the future.

Winston Burdett's elegant voice was first heard on CBS covering the German invasion of Norway in April 1940. A man who'd finished Harvard in three years and graduated *summa cum laude* in Romance languages, Burdett had been a stringer in Europe for the *Brooklyn Eagle*.

CBS also was expanding its news operation in New York. John Daly, Ned Calmer, and Douglas Edwards joined Robert Trout to form a most impressive group of newscasters.

The network needed these pros to keep up with an ever-expanding war. On a single day — May 10, 1940 — the Luftwaffe bombed Belgium, Holland, and

Luxembourg. Chamberlain resigned that day and was replaced by Winston Churchill. Breckinridge was the first to broadcast the capitulation of Belgium, and Sevareid was first to report both the German end-run around the Maginot Line and the fall of France.

The Sevareids' experience during the rapid French collapse mirrored the Shirers' ordeal two years earlier in Vienna. Lois Sevareid had an extremely difficult pregnancy, gaining a hundred pounds and being forced to lie still in a bed for three months. Upon delivering twins, she saw her husband dash off to report the German advance. When Eric returned to the hospital, he found it empty of doctors, staff, and patients, save Lois, immobile with her babies. Everyone else had fled the Nazis.

Sevareid, Grandin, and LeSueur were torn. They didn't want to abandon their posts, but two of them had families to think about. LeSueur tried to board a troop ship for Britain but was refused. Then he watched as a German plane bombed that very ship, killing thousands. LeSueur found another way to get to London.

Tom Grandin was a newlywed. His Romanian-born wife was pregnant, did not speak English, had no passport, and although she was booked on the SS *Washington*, bound for the United States, she would not be admitted without him. At the last second, he decided to board with her and leave CBS.

Sevareid, saying good-bye to a suddenly mid-sized family bound for the States, must have been tempted to follow Grandin's example. Instead, he crossed to England, worried that he had let Murrow down by leaving the Continent in the face of the Nazi advance. Aboard ship, he heard William L. Shirer reporting on the French surrender.

Shirer was unhappy in Berlin, having the post-*Anschluss* blues and sorry to return to the daily diet of Nazi lies. He almost turned down the opportunity to cover Hitler's further humiliation of the French. The signing took place at Compiègne, in the very railroad car where Germany had been forced to sign the World War I surrender. Hitler had ordered all accounts of the surrender to be broadcast later from Berlin. Shirer tried to reach New York anyway. A technician in Berlin mistakenly sent Shirer's report to New York, where it was picked up by CBS. Shirer's story beat the rest of the world by nearly six hours. It was Shirer's biggest exclusive.

Arriving in England, Sevareid called Murrow in London and feared he might be fired. He need not have worried. Murrow was delighted to hear from him and urged him, "Come to London. There's work to be done here."

He lost Mary Marvin Breckinridge, however, when she left CBS in June to marry a career diplomat, Jefferson Patterson, who was stationed in Berlin.

Hitler spent the summer of 1940 consolidating his gains. Almost all of Europe belonged to the Third Reich. There remained those pesky British Isles, and he was confident they would soon be his. The summer bombing of England escalated dramatically on August 24.

Initially, the bombing targeted airfields and other military and shipping targets along the English coast and was to be a prelude to a planned invasion called Operation Sea Lion. The Royal Air Force countered so well in the next two weeks that the invasion never was launched. On September 7, Murrow and two other reporters drove to the mouth of the Thames in southeastern England and parked near a haystack to observe the air war. Lying on their backs against the hay, they watched the German bombers arrive and the Spitfires and Hurricanes climb up to meet them. There were many more German planes that night, and the reporters needn't have left home to see them. The planes followed the Thames west and bombed London.

The bombing of the docks of East London killed many hundreds among the working-class people who lived there, and the champions of the master race might have been smart to keep pounding that area to exploit the British class system. In time, the bombs fell also on dukes and earls, even on Buckingham Palace. The queen almost was relieved at that, saying that at last she could look East Londoners in the face. Parliament was bombed, as were Big Ben and the British Museum. St. Paul's was one of the few great landmarks spared.

Broadcasting House, considered by Germany a military target, was bombed several times. This was the BBC facility that also was used by CBS and NBC reporters who broadcast from the building's subbasement. Murrow and NBC's Fred Bate were there when Broadcasting House took a direct hit from a bomb that lodged in the center of the building. The UXB (unexploded bomb) experts were at work when the bomb ultimately went off, killing seven and destroying the BBC's program library.

Another bomb nearly killed Bate as he neared Broadcasting House. The blast tore off part of his ear and embedded shrapnel in his head. Although the tendons of both legs were severed, Bate, script still in hand, crawled toward the building, intent on delivering his broadcast. He was sent back to the United States to recover. Competitors, Bate and Murrow often had covered stories together and were good friends.

CBS suffered no casualties during the Blitz, although three successive offices were destroyed. On one occasion, Kay Campbell was blasted across the room and under a rug. Ed and Janet Murrow had several close calls, and the fire from one explosion reached the building next to their flat. That was the night Ed wanted to stop at the Devonshire Arms for a drink with his BBC pals who were regulars at the pub, but Janet insisted he walk her home. So they passed it by and missed the bomb that reduced the Devonshire Arms to rubble.

Ed wanted his listeners to hear the sounds of war. For a special program called "London after Dark," he left the studio and went to Trafalgar Square, stood at St. Martin in the Fields church, and put his microphone on the ground to pick up the sounds of people walking to bomb shelters, "like ghosts shod with steel shoes." He wanted to show there was no panic in London.

Gathering sound is now routine in radio, but not in Murrow's day, when the networks banned recording of any sort. The theory was that recordings defeated the purpose of networks. The networks carried live broadcasts by the best orchestras. If a network played recordings by those orchestras it would be doing nothing more than its affiliated stations could do for themselves. So the networks permitted no recordings, and the sounds of World War II could be heard only if a reporter happened to be broadcasting from the scene of conflict. Ed Murrow would have to leave the subbasement of the BBC's Broadcasting House if his listeners were going to hear the war.

Ed wanted to string wires to the roof of Broadcasting House and describe a German air raid in progress. The British government feared the Luftwaffe would pick up his report and use it as a measure of their success or as a guide to desired targets. Another possibility was that it might pinpoint Broadcasting House as a target. Ultimately the government determined that Ed's reports of a brave Britain standing alone against the Nazis despite the Blitz was just what London wanted Americans to hear and might galvanize some support from Washington. He was given some rules and permission to do a trial run from the roof of a building several blocks away.

Murrow's first live rooftop broadcast (see the introduction) was made on September 21, 1940. The bombing was heavy that night but, by good luck or bad, it stopped just a minute before Ed began his broadcast. Still, listeners could hear the antiaircraft guns and the whistles of either police officers or air-raid wardens. They were not referees' whistles, but the reedy, chordlike shriek of a European police whistle. Ed doesn't sound like he's reading, working instead from ad-lib description and some notes he'd prepared on what he'd seen in the neighborhood earlier in the day. He is generous with metaphors and rich with description: ". . . that faint-red, angry snap of antiaircraft bursts against the steel-blue sky . . . the sound of guns off in the distance very faintly, like someone kicking a tub . . . four searchlights reach up, disappear in the light of a three-quarter moon." Newsreel footage of the Blitz is in black-and-white; Ed's radio reports were in color.

The rooftop reports were dramatic, but Ed's studio broadcasts are still fascinating to read, all the more so because he never actually wrote them down. Ed noticed that BBC reporters didn't write; they dictated their scripts to someone who would transcribe them. Ed, a former speech major, copied that practice and dictated a narrative to Kay Campbell, who then wrote his script. The result is a text that looks awkward on the page and doesn't always follow the rules of grammar, but sounds stunning when spoken by Murrow.

Listeners came to expect the unexpected of a Murrow broadcast, which might relate the day's debate in Parliament, examine British wartime policy, or simply be an account of what Ed had seen that day in the streets of London. He was easily capable of presenting the big picture of Churchill, Parliament, and the king, but he was absolutely magnificent in portraying the little picture of pensioners, merchants, and shopgirls. His style was not the third-person journalism of today. He delivered personal essays, rich in word pictures, of the everyday bloke on the street muddling through his worst nightmare. Ed had an eye for the lone policeman standing vigil at an unexploded bomb, relieving his boredom by repeatedly tossing his whistle into the air and catching it, or the struggle of a young woman with the steering wheel of her ambulance. He was giving the United States his fanfare for the common man by focusing on stubborn British resistance:

One night I stood in front of a smashed grocery store and heard a dripping inside. It was the only sound in all London. Two cans of peaches had been drilled clean through by flying glass, and the juice was dripping down onto the floor. . . .

There was a flower shop in the East End. Nearly every other building in the block had been smashed. There was a funeral wreath in the window of the shop — price: three shillings and sixpence, less than a dollar. In front of Buckingham Palace there's a bed of red and white flowers — untouched — the reddest flowers I've ever seen. . . .

Today I went to buy a hat — my favorite shop had gone, blown to bits. The windows of my shoe store were blown out. I decided to have a haircut; the windows of the barbershop were gone, but the Italian barber was still doing business. Someday, he said, we smile again, but the food it doesn't taste so good since being bombed. I went on to another shop to buy some flashlight batteries. The clerk said: "You needn't buy so many. We'll have enough for the whole winter." But I said: "What if you aren't here?" There were buildings down in that street, and he replied: "Of course, we'll be here. We've been in business here for a hundred and fifty years. . . ."

In one window — or what used to be a window — was a sign. It read: Shattered but Not Shuttered. Nearby was another shop, displaying a crudely lettered sign reading: Knocked but Not Locked. They were both doing business in the open air. Halfway down the block there was a desk on the sidewalk. A man sat behind it with a pile of notes at his elbow. He was paying off the staff of the store — the store that stood there yesterday.

It was not all grit and pluck, of course, and he didn't shrink from describing what bombs can do. He told of seeing "a man pinned under wreckage where a broken gas main sears his arm and face" and "human beings, looking like broken, castaway, dust-covered barrels, being lifted . . . out of . . . the basement of a bombed-out house." Ed interviewed a British bomber pilot who flinched at the sound of a falling bomb; it was his first time being on the receiving end. The pilot was horrified that he probably was causing the same death and destruction in Germany that he was seeing for the first time in London.

Although Ed dined and drank with the swells, he remained the working-class son of the logging camps. He said that "the intellectual . . . counts for even less than he did a year ago; the man who can run a lathe, fly a plane, or build a ship counts for more." There also was this gem:

We looked in on a renowned Mayfair hotel tonight and found many old dowagers and retired colonels settling back on the overstuffed settees in the lobby. It was not the sort of protection I'd seek from a direct hit from a half-ton bomb, but if you were a retired colonel and his lady you might feel that the risk was worth it because you would at least be bombed with the right sort of people, and you could always get a drink if you were a resident of the hotel.

Ed avoided bomb shelters except to report about them. He was afraid he'd grow accustomed to them. Instead, he drove through London in an open car (the better to see all around him) or walked the streets with the equally fearless Larry LeSueur, whose carefree personality suited him better than that of the brooding Eric Sevareid. Sevareid longed to be as close to Ed as LeSueur, but he understood Ed's need to be around someone who didn't flinch as the bombs fell. Sevareid had enough of the Blitz after just one month and returned to his family in the United States in September 1940.

William L. Shirer left Berlin for New York in December, ending fifteen years as a foreign correspondent. He smuggled his diary past the Nazis, burying it in a trunk beneath stacks of his CBS scripts. *Berlin Diary* was an instant best seller in 1941. Both Shirer and Sevareid discovered on their return home that the CBS European reporters were radio stars. They also had difficulty coming to grips with American isolation as the Nazis conquered much of Europe.

The Murrow broadcasts addressed the comfort of Americans on the sidelines as Hitler pummeled the British. "You will have no dawn raid as we shall probably have. . . . Your families are not scattered by the winds of war." Ed certainly didn't mind making his listeners feel guilty. The loss of more than forty-three thousand British lives to German bombs in a twelve-month period would test anyone's objectivity. The broadcasts were effective in terms of government policy, too. When President Roosevelt's envoy Harry Hopkins visited London in January 1941, it was Murrow he wanted to see. Ed thought Hopkins was going to give him an exclusive interview, but Hopkins asked all the questions. Three months later, Congress passed the Lend-Lease Act, and U.S. neutrality was over. Privately, Churchill gave the credit to Murrow's broadcasts.

Janet Murrow also broadcast for CBS during this period and was active as a leader of "Bundles for Britain," which channeled private American assistance to the British. Janet had to try to sleep while bombs were falling and her husband was broadcasting in the wee hours of the morning (evening in New York). She also had to manage a household that was part salon, part chowhouse, as the Murrow apartment became a gathering place for journalists, exiles, diplomats, politicians, visiting Americans, and bombed-out friends. For a time it was the CBS London bureau when the network office was bombed. Harold Laski was a regular and so was Jan Masaryk, Czechoslovakia's foreign minister in exile.

Operation Sea Lion never took place because a German invasion depended on air superiority that never was achieved. Berlin kept trying, though, beginning incendiary bombing on May 10, a night of two thousand fires. More than two thousand Britons were killed that night, but the country would not surrender. Murrow marveled that the democratic process continued to function, and to the extent it was possible, so did everyday life. "My own apartment is in one of the most heavily bombed areas of London, but the newspapers are on the doorstep each morning. So is the bottle of milk." Britain finally got some relief the next month when Germany shifted its attention to the east and invaded the Soviet Union.

The Overseas Press Club honored Ed's reporting of the Blitz, but it deserved so much more. It remains some of the finest journalism and radio ever done. Ed earned numerous awards for his later wartime reporting; some of them were make-goods for not recognizing his superior reporting of 1940 and 1941.

In September, Ed received word that Ida Lou Anderson had died. He had seen so much of death in London and had attended the funerals of close friends, but the passing of his young mentor from Pullman made him cry.

In the final months of 1941, Larry Le-Sueur left London to cover the fighting in Russia, and Cecil Brown, the CBS reporter in Singapore, nearly died at sea. Brown was aboard a British cruiser, the HMS *Repulse*, torpedoed and sunk by Japanese planes. His reporting of that story resulted in Headliner, Peabody, and Overseas Press Club awards, a $1,000 bonus, a best-selling book, and a sponsored CBS newscast slot in New York.

Murrow wanted to add Helen Kirkpatrick of the *Chicago Daily News* to the CBS war reporting staff, but Ed Klauber ordered him not to hire any more female reporters. Instead, Murrow stole a pair of

Rhodes scholars from United Press, Murrow's favorite news organization to raid. Charles Collingwood, a Cornell alumnus, was a project for Murrow. Collingwood later became a legend for both his lifestyle and his skill at a microphone. Howard K. Smith, who'd been a champion hurdler at Tulane, was given a farewell party by colleagues in Berlin before leaving to assume his CBS post in Switzerland. He had such a drunken good time that he decided to stick around for a few days. Luckily for Smith, his pals forced him onto the train and waved good-bye. It was the last train on which an American was allowed to leave Berlin. The date was December 7, 1941.

5

Over Berlin

The Battle of Britain was won and Ed Murrow sailed home, arriving in New York on November 24, 1941. He learned almost immediately what a celebrity he'd become. On December 2, William Paley gave him a testimonial dinner at the Waldorf-Astoria, where eleven hundred VIPs rose in a standing ovation after hearing poet Archibald Mac-Leish pay tribute to Ed:

> You laid the dead of London at our doors and we knew that the dead were our dead . . . without more emotion than needed be . . . you have destroyed the superstition that what is done beyond three thousand miles of water is not really done at all. There were some people in this country who did not want the people of America to hear the things you had to say.

It was not a night for isolationists.

On Sunday, December 7, Ed was playing golf at Burning Tree Country Club in a Maryland suburb of Washington, D.C., when he learned about Pearl Harbor. Janet called the White House, expecting to hear that their scheduled dinner with the Roosevelts that evening was canceled. "We all have to eat," said Mrs. Roosevelt. "Come anyway."

The Murrows dined with Eleanor Roosevelt, Ed catching glimpses of top State and War Department officials passing by on their way to see the president. Afterward Ed was asked to wait, and Janet returned to their hotel. It was past midnight when Ed was shown into the Oval Office. The public still didn't know the extent of the damage to the Pacific Fleet, but FDR gave Ed a full briefing, which included news of the destruction of U.S. planes "on the ground, by God, on the ground!" Some doubted that FDR was surprised by the Japanese attack, but Murrow believed the president and his men had no warning. He said they were brilliant actors if they were lying. Leaving the White House, Ed was uncertain whether he'd just received privileged information. He decided he had — and did not report his exclusive. The next day, he sat in the House gallery and heard FDR ask for a declaration of war.

The Murrows spent the winter on the lecture circuit, with proceeds going to British War Relief. There were reunions with Bill Shirer and with the Murrows of North Carolina and Washington, plus a triumphal return to his alma mater, Washington State in Pullman. Simon & Schuster published an anthology of his broadcasts, titled *This Is London*. Crowds packed the lecture halls to see this new phenomenon, a radio star journalist on his national victory lap.

Ed and Janet returned to London in April and found that there were now many more Americans in the city. Ed was the man the British asked about these new American allies and the man the Americans asked about their new British hosts. Paley visited in August and was newly impressed with the range of contacts his European director enjoyed.

Bill Downs was added to the CBS reporting team and sent to Moscow to replace Larry LeSueur, who rotated to Cairo. Once again, Ed stuck to his hiring pattern, since Downs had been a United Press reporter in Kansas City, Denver, and

New York before an assignment in London. A good writer with marginal vocal qualities, Downs also spun entertaining tales over drinks.

Charles Collingwood was assigned to cover the fighting in North Africa. Although he was considered green before this assignment, Collingwood demonstrated great skill in his reporting and enterprise in beating the competition. His work in North Africa earned him a George Foster Peabody Award.

On December 13, 1942, Ed told his listeners what he'd heard about the Nazis' "final solution":

One is almost stunned into silence by some of the information reaching London. Some of it is months old, but it's eyewitness stuff supported by a wealth of detail and vouched for by responsible governments . . . millions of human beings, most of them Jews, are being gathered up with ruthless efficiency and murdered . . . a picture of mass murder and moral depravity unequaled in the history of the world.

Then he told about atrocities in Holland and Norway, and the deportations of Jews from the Warsaw Ghetto to Treblinka, where survivors of the trip were killed. He put this on the record two-and-a-half years before the camps were liberated.

In March 1943 Ed went to North Africa and saw his first ground combat, coming under fire in Tunisia and telling listeners about the aftermath:

Where the road cuts down to meet the stream there is a knocked-out tank, two dead men beside it, and two more digging a grave. A little farther along a German soldier sits smiling against the bank. He is covered with dust and he is dead. On the rising ground beyond, a British lieutenant lies with his head on his arm as though shielding himself from the wind. He is dead, too.

Upon returning to London, Ed received an unusually tempting offer to become the programming chief of the BBC. Churchill himself wanted Ed for the job. Ed traveled home to the United States, called on President Roosevelt at the White House, and stopped by to see Supreme Court justice Felix Frankfurter, an old friend from his IIE days when Frankfurter was a Harvard law professor. Frankfurter urged him to take the BBC job, but Ed was amused to think of the reverse situation — a Brit being allowed to run an American network. (Decades later, British-born Howard Stringer would be president of CBS.) Ed decided not to take the job. After seeing doctors about his continuing pulmonary problems, he sailed back to England aboard the *Queen Elizabeth* along with fifteen thousand U.S. servicemen heading off to war.

Murrow, still trying to recruit the best talent, attempted another raid on United Press, offering a job to a very able war correspondent named Walter Cronkite. But UP countered with a $25-a-week raise and promises that Cronkite would be their star. Cronkite handed Murrow a rare rejection that Ed never forgot and never forgave.

On August 6, 1943, CBS announced the retirement of Bill Paley's deputy, Ed Klauber, due to illness. Klauber had looked fine when Ed saw him the previous month in New York. Paley must have had enough of Klauber's abrasiveness, and replaced him with Paul Kesten. Klauber went to Washington to run the Office of War Information. His departure from CBS was a blow to Murrow, who had enjoyed total support from Klauber, the man who had hired him. Klauber had been a journalist and had hired Paul White to establish CBS News. Kesten's background was not in news. At least Ed could take comfort in his close relationship with Paley.

Eric Sevareid spent that month trying to reach China, a country with two armies opposed to Japanese occupiers. Sevareid ultimately would find that the Communists were a more determined force than the official Chinese army, but on the way there, the C-46 in which he was traveling developed engine trouble. Sevareid, who previously had been squeamish about danger, managed to overcome his fears and bail out over Burma before his plane crashed. The survivors enjoyed the hospitality of a tribe of headhunters until a British agent showed up to lead them on a 120-mile march into India and civilization.

A month later, Cecil Brown remarked in his newscast that Americans were losing enthusiasm for the war. Paul White was furious, declaring that Brown had no right to inject his opinion into a CBS newscast. Brown had many defenders, but Bill Shirer took the side of his employer, a position that probably haunted him a few years later when he found himself in the same position. The conflict between CBS and Brown escalated, and Brown resigned. The hero of Singapore coverage in 1941 was no longer part of the CBS team.

As 1943 came to a close, Ed Murrow found the opportunity he'd been seeking for a year. Having endured all those German bombs over Britain, Murrow was anxious to witness British bombs being dropped on Germany. By coin toss, others had been selected before him to fly aboard British bombers making runs over Berlin. On December 2, 1943, he finally got his chance. Secrecy was important, and Janet was kept in the dark as Ed simply disappeared for several days. Afterward he reported: "Last night some young gentlemen of the RAF took me to Berlin." He was aboard a Lancaster bomber code-named *D for Dog*.

Yesterday afternoon, the waiting was over. The weather was right; the target was to be the big city. The crew captains walked into the briefing room, looked at the maps and charts, and sat down with their big celluloid pads on their knees. The atmosphere was that of a school and a church. The weathermen gave us the weather. The pilots were reminded that Berlin is Germany's greatest center of war production. The intelligence officer told us how many heavy and light ack-ack guns, how many searchlights we might expect to encounter. Then Jock, the wing commander, explained the system of markings, the kind of flare that would be used by the Pathfinders. He said that concentration was the secret of success in these raids, that as long as the aircraft stayed well bunched, they would protect each other. The captains of the aircraft marched out.

I noticed that the big Canadian with the slow, easy grin had printed "Berlin" at the top of his pad and then embellished it with a scroll. The redheaded English boy with the two-weeks'-old mustache was the last to leave the room. Late in the afternoon we went to the locker room to draw parachutes, Mae Wests, and all the rest. As we dressed, a couple of the Australians were whistling. Walking out to the bus that was to take us to the aircraft, I heard the station loudspeakers announcing that that evening all personnel would be able to see a film, *Star Spangled Rhythm*, free.

We went out and stood around a big, black, four-motored Lancaster, *D for Dog*. A small station wagon delivered a thermos bottle of coffee, chewing gum, an orange, and a bit of chocolate for each man. Up in that part of England the air hums and throbs with the sound of aircraft motors all day. But for half an hour before takeoff, the skies are dead, silent, and expectant. A lone hawk hovered over the airfield, absolutely still as he faced into the wind. Jack, the tail gunner, said, "It would be nice if *we* could fly like that."

D for Dog eased around the perimeter track to the end of the runway. We sat there for a moment. The green light flashed and we were rolling — ten seconds ahead of schedule! The takeoff was smooth as silk. The wheels came up, and *D for Dog* started the long climb. As we came up through the clouds, I looked right and left and counted fourteen black Lancasters climbing for the place where men must burn oxygen to live. The sun was going down, and its red glow made rivers and lakes of fire on tops of the clouds. Down to the southward, the clouds piled up to form castles, battlements, and whole cities, all tinged with red.

Soon we were out over the North Sea. Dave, the navigator, asked Jock if he couldn't make a little more speed. We were nearly two minutes late. By this time we were all using oxygen. The talk on the intercom was brief and crisp. Everyone sounded relaxed. For a while, the eight of us in our little world in exile moved over the sea. There was a quarter moon on the starboard beam. Jock's quiet voice came through on the intercom, "That'll be flak ahead." We were approaching the enemy coast. The flak looked like a cigarette lighter in a dark room — one that won't light. Sparks but no flame. The sparks crackling just above the level of the cloudtops. We flew steady and straight, and soon the flak was directly below us.

D-Dog rocked a little from right to left, but that wasn't caused by the flak. We were in the slipstream of other Lancasters ahead, and we were over the enemy coast. And then a strange thing happened. The aircraft seemed to grow smaller. Jack, in the rear turret, Wally, the mid-upper gunner; Titch, the wireless operator — all seemed somehow to draw closer to Jock in the cockpit. It was as though each man's shoulder was against the other's. The understanding was complete. The intercom came to life, and Jock said, "Two aircraft on the port beam." Jack, in the tail, said, "Okay, sir, they're Lancs." The whole crew was a unit and wasn't wasting words.

The cloud below was ten tenths. The blue-green jet of the exhausts licked back along the leading edge, and there were other aircraft all around us. The whole great aerial armada was hurtling toward Berlin. We flew so for twenty minutes, when Jock looked up at a vapor trail curling across above us, remarking in a conversational tone that from the look of it he thought there was a fighter up there. Occasionally the angry red of ack-ack burst through the clouds, but it was far away, and we took only academic interest. We were flying in the third wave. Jock asked Wally in the mid-upper turret and Jack in the rear turret if they were cold. They said they were all right, and thanked him for asking. Even asked how I was, and I said, "All right, so far." The cloud was beginning to thin out. Up to the north we could see light, and the flak began to liven up ahead of it.

Boz, the bomb aimer, crackled through on the intercom, "There's a battle going on on the starboard beam." We couldn't see the aircraft, but we could see the jets of red tracer being exchanged. Suddenly there was a burst of yellow flame, and Jock remarked, "That's a fighter going down. Note the position." The whole thing was interesting, but remote. Dave, the navigator, who was sitting back with his maps, charts, and compasses, said, "The attack ought to begin in exactly two minutes." We were still over the clouds. But suddenly those dirty gray clouds turned white. We were over the outer searchlight defenses. The clouds below us were white, and we were black. *D-Dog* seemed like a black bug on a white sheet. The flak began coming up, but none of it close. We were still a long way from Berlin. I didn't realize just how far.

Jock observed, "There's a kite on fire dead ahead." It was a great, slow-moving meteor slanting toward the earth. By this time we were about thirty miles from our target area in Berlin. That thirty miles was the longest flight I have ever made. Dead on time, Boz, the bomb aimer, reported, "Target indicators going down." The same moment the sky ahead was lit up by bright yellow flares. Off to starboard, another kite went down in flames. The flares were sprouting all over the sky — reds and greens and yellows — and we were flying straight for the center of the fireworks. *D-Dog* seemed to be closing in. The clouds had cleared, and off to the starboard a Lanc was caught by at least fourteen searchlight beams. We could see him twist and turn and finally break out. But still the whole thing had a quality of unreality about it. No one seemed to be shooting at us, but it was getting lighter all the time. Suddenly a tremendous big blob of yellow light appeared dead ahead, another to the right, and another to the left. We were flying straight for them.

Jock pointed out to me the dummy fires and flares to the right and left. But we kept going in. Dead ahead there was a whole chain of flares looking like stoplights. Another Lanc was coned on our starboard beam. The lights seemed to be supporting it. Again we could see those little bubbles of colored light driving at it from two sides. The German fighters were at him. And then, with no warning at all, *D-Dog* was filled with an unhealthy white light. I was standing just behind Jock and could see all the seams on the wings. His quiet Scots voice beat into my ears, "Steady, lads, we've been coned." His slender body lifted half out of his seat as he jammed the control column forward and to the left. We were going down.

Jock was wearing woolen gloves with the fingers cut off. I could see his fingernails turn white as he gripped the wheel. And then I was on my knees, flat on the deck, for he had whipped the *Dog* back into a climbing turn. The knees should have been strong enough to support me, but they weren't, and the stomach seemed to be in some danger of letting me down, too. I picked myself up and looked out again. It seemed that one big searchlight, instead of being twenty thousand feet below, was mounted right on our wingtip. *D-Dog* was corkscrewing. As we rolled down on the other side, I began to see what was happening to Berlin.

The clouds were gone and the sticks of incendiaries from the preceding waves made the place look like a badly laid out city with the streetlights on. The small incendiaries were going down like a fistful of white rice thrown on a piece of black velvet. As Jock hauled the *Dog* up again, I was thrown to the other side of the cockpit, and there below were more incendiaries, glowing white and then turning red. The cookies — the four-thousand-pound high explosives — were bursting below like great sunflowers gone mad. And then, as we started down again, still held in the lights, I remembered that the *Dog* still had one of those cookies and a whole basket of incendiaries in his belly, and the lights still held us. And I was very frightened.

While Jock was flinging him about in the air, he suddenly flung over the intercom, "Two aircraft on the port beam." I looked astern and saw Wally, the mid-upper, whip his turret around to port and then look up to see a single-engine fighter slide just above us. The other aircraft was one of ours. Finally, we were out of the cone, flying level. I looked down, and the white fires had turned red. They were beginning to merge and spread, just like butter does on a hot plate. Jock and Boz, the bomb aimer, began to discuss the target. The smoke was getting thick down below. Boz said he liked the two green flares on the ground almost dead ahead. He began calling his directions. And just then a new bunch of big flares went down on the far side of the sea of flame and flare that seemed to be directly below us. He thought that would be a better aiming point. Jock agreed, and we flew on. The bomb doors were open. Boz called his directions, "Five left, five left." And then there was a gentle, confident, upward thrust under my feet, and Boz said, "Cookie gone." A few seconds later, the incendiaries went, and *D-Dog* seemed lighter and easier to handle.

I thought I could make out the outline of the streets below. But the bomb aimer didn't agree, and he ought to know. By this time, all those patches of white on black had turned yellow and started to flow together. Another searchlight caught us but didn't hold us. Then through the intercom came the word, "One can of incendiaries didn't clear. We're still carrying it." And Jock replied, "Is it a big one or a little one?" The word came back, "Little one, I think, but I'm not sure. I'll check." More of those yellow flares came down and hung about us. I haven't seen so much light since the war began. Finally the intercom announced that it was only a small can of incendiaries left, and Jock remarked, "Well, it's hardly worth going back and doing another run-up for that." If there had been a good fat bundle left, he would have gone back through that stuff and done it all over again.

I began to breathe and to reflect again — that all men would be brave if only they could leave their stomachs at home. Then there was a tremendous whoomp, an unintelligible shout from the tail gunner, and *D-Dog* shivered and lost altitude. I looked to the port side, and there was a Lancaster that seemed close enough to touch. He had whipped straight under us, missed us by twenty-five, fifty feet, no one knew how much. The navigator sang out the new course, and we were heading for home. Jock was doing what I had heard him tell his pilots to do so often — flying dead on course. He flew straight into a huge green searchlight and, as he rammed the throttles home, remarked, "We'll have a little trouble getting away from this one." And again, *D-Dog* dove, climbed, and twisted, and was finally free. We flew level then. I looked on the port beam at the target area. There was a sullen, obscene glare. The fires seemed to have found each other — and we were heading home.

For a little while it was smooth sailing. We saw more battles. Then another plane in flames, but no one could tell whether it was ours or theirs. We were still near the target. Dave, the navigator, said, "Hold her steady, skipper. I want to get an astral site." And Jock held her steady. And the flak began coming up at us. It seemed to be very close. It was winking off both wings. But the *Dog* was steady. Finally Dave said, "Okay, skipper, thank you very much." And a great orange blob of flak smacked up just in front of us. And Jock said, "I think they're shooting at us." I'd thought so for some time.

And he began to throw *D for Dog* up, around, and about again. And when we were clear of the barrage, I asked him how close the bursts were and he said, "Not very close. When they're really near, you can smell 'em." That proved nothing, for I'd been holding my breath. Jack sang out from the rear turret, said his oxygen was getting low, thought maybe the lead had frozen. Titch, the wireless operator, went scrambling back with a new mask and a bottle of oxygen. Dave, the navigator, said, "We're crossing the coast." My mind went back to the time I crossed that coast in 1938, in a plane that had taken off from Prague. Just ahead of me sat two refugees from Vienna — an old man and his wife. The copilot came back and told them that we were outside German territory. The old man reached out and grasped his wife's hand. The work that was done last night was a massive blow of retribution for all those who have fled from the sounds of shots and blows on the stricken Continent.

We began to lose height over the North Sea. We were over England's shore. The land was dark beneath us. Somewhere down there below, American boys were probably bombing-up Fortresses and Liberators, getting ready for the day's work. We were over the home field. We called the control tower, and the calm, clear voice of an English girl replied, "Greetings, *D-Dog*. You are diverted to Mule Bag." We swung around, contacted Mule Bag, came in on the flare path, touched down very gently, ran along the end of the runway, and turned left. And Jock, the finest pilot in Bomber Command, said to the control tower, "*D-Dog* clear of runway."

When we went in for interrogation, I looked on the board and saw that the big, slow-smiling Canadian and the redheaded English boy with the two-weeks-old mustache hadn't made it.

They were missing. There were four reporters on this operation — two of them didn't come back. Two friends of mine — Norman Stockton, of Australian Associated Newspapers, and Lowell Bennett, an American representing International News Service. There is something of a tradition amongst reporters that those of us who are prevented by circumstances from filing their stories will be covered by their colleagues. This has been my effort to do so. [Bennett actually parachuted that night and was a German prisoner until May 1945.]

In the aircraft in which I flew, the men who flew and fought it poured into my ears their comments on fighters, flak, and flares in the same tones they would have used in reporting a host of daffodils. I have no doubt that Bennett and Stockton would have given you a better account of last night's activities.

Berlin was a kind of orchestrated hell, a terrible symphony of light and flame. It isn't a pleasant kind of warfare — the men doing it speak of it as a job. Yesterday afternoon, when the tapes were stretched out on the big map all the way to Berlin and back again, a young pilot with old eyes said to me, "I see that we are working again tonight." That's the frame of mind in which the job is being done. The job isn't pleasant; it's terribly tiring. Men die in the sky while others are roasted alive in their cellars. Berlin last night wasn't a pretty sight. In about thirty-five minutes it was hit with about three times the amount of stuff that ever came down on London in a night-long Blitz. This is a calculated, remorseless campaign of destruction. Right now the mechanics are probably working on *D-Dog*, getting him ready to fly again.

Today, a radio story like that one would be heavy with sound. We would hear the drone of the engines, the snap of the flak, the conversations of the crew, and perhaps some exclamations from the reporter. With a ban on the use of recordings, Ed Murrow's account of *D for Dog* making an orchestrated hell of Berlin had to rely on word pictures to help us experience what it was like to be on that mission. Had he the use of ambient sound, the images in his narrative would likely have been less vivid. The broadcast earned him his first Peabody Award.

Paul White had forbidden Murrow from flying on combat missions because he believed the CBS European director was too valuable to the company to be put at such risk. Although Ed always promised White that he would stop, he totaled twenty-five combat missions before the war was over.

In 1944, Ed was made president of the American Foreign Correspondents Association in London. He had tried to join the group in 1937 when he first arrived in England, but he had not even been allowed to attend its meetings. What did radio have to do with journalism? Thanks to Ed Murrow, radio now had a lot to do with journalism.

6

Buchenwald

The last of the wartime staff who came to be known as Murrow's Boys was yet another United Press reporter. Richard C. Hottelet had been a philosophy major at Brooklyn College and had hoped to continue his studies in Berlin. German universities of 1937 were more concerned with Hitler and Hess than with Goethe and Kant, so Hottelet joined Howard K. Smith at the UP's Berlin bureau. Hottelet covered the occupation of the Sudetenland and the German blitzkrieg all across western Europe to Dunkirk. He and the Nazis hated each other, and Hottelet was imprisoned as a spy. Four months later, he was exchanged for a German being held by the United States. After a stint with the Office of War Information, he joined CBS just in time for planning coverage of D-Day, the Allied landing in northern France.

Murrow followed orders from White to

remain in London and let his reporters cover D-Day. Hottelet was with the Ninth Air Force, which bombed German gun positions in Normandy. He was the only CBS D-Day reporter heard on June 6 or for several days thereafter. Bill Downs landed with British troops. Larry LeSueur had to spend two days with seasick GI's, bobbing aboard a landing craft in the English Channel. LeSueur saw the most combat, running across Utah Beach and taking cover at the seawall, then witnessing the brutal hedgerow fighting that followed in the next few days. The Germans were still shooting when Charles Collingwood landed on the beach hours after the first troops went ashore. Collingwood recorded a broadcast on the beach and hoped that CBS would make an exception to its ban on recording. He was back in London three days later, and the network did indeed play his recording — many times. Downs and LeSueur were not heard from because of a breakdown in the military's system of handling broadcast reports. Until a transmitter could be set up, the plan was to have the reporters make their way back to the beach and hand their stories to the military for delivery to London. Some reporters made the dangerous trip twice a day, but the stories never reached London. LeSuour didn't get to tell his D-Day story until mid-June.

Eric Sevareid, who had covered the fall of France, now covered some of its liberation, moving with the Seventh Army from the Riviera through the Rhône Valley before returning to London.

Collingwood was so determined to be the first reporter to announce the liberation of Paris that he did so forty-eight hours before it happened. He sent a report declaring that a French armored division and a popular uprising had retaken Paris. Military censors in London were instructed to hold the report until the event occurred. Collingwood figured a report already cleared by censors would give him an edge over the competition. A freak series of events resulted in the report being broadcast on August 23, 1944, while ten thousand German troops remained in Paris. Celebrations broke out in world capitals; heads of state sent congratulations to one another. Collingwood had made one of the biggest blunders in journalism history, and although many a reporter has been fired for far less, Collingwood had Murrow's backing and remained with CBS for many years. When

Paris was actually liberated, on the twenty-fifth, Larry LeSueur was the first radio correspondent to report the news, but only because he went directly to a transmitter and didn't bother clearing his story through the censors. The military briefly suspended LeSueur.

When Collingwood reached a free Paris, the city liberated him. Always a man who enjoyed the good life, Collingwood remained in Paris and enjoyed its charms while LeSueur, Downs, Hottelet, and Howard K. Smith covered the Allied advance.

Hottelet was the first to report the Battle of the Bulge, and he was the first CBS reporter to enter Germany in 1945. Then in March, he was aboard a B-17 hit by anti-aircraft fire over Germany, but the pilot pointed the plane toward the Rhine, and Hottelet was still over Germany when he and others finally bailed out. Later, when U.S. troops hooked up with Russian forces at the Elbe, Hottelet was there.

Downs came under heavy fire in France, Belgium, and Holland. Diving into a ditch for cover one day, he told the UP's Walter Cronkite, "Just think. If we survive them, these will be the good old days."

The war in Europe was winding down,

and Ed Murrow longed for a final bit of action. He joined Collingwood in covering General George Patton's Third Army in Germany. On April 11, the correspondents had a night of poker, and Murrow was the big winner, stuffing bills into every pocket of his uniform. The next day, the troops liberated the Nazi concentration camp at Buchenwald, and Collingwood watched Murrow empty his pockets, giving away his money to the survivors. Murrow was so overwhelmed by what he saw at Buchenwald that he let the other reporters break the news of the camp's liberation. (The big story that day, however, was the death of Franklin Roosevelt.) Three days later, when he was back in London, Ed found the words:

Permit me to tell you what you would have seen, and heard, had you been with me on Thursday. It will not be pleasant listening. If you are at lunch, or if you have no appetite to hear what Germans have done, now is a good time to switch off the radio, for I propose to tell you of Buchenwald. It is on a small hill about four miles outside Weimar, and it was one of the largest concentration camps in Germany, and it was built to last. As we approached it, we saw about a hundred men in civilian clothes with rifles advancing in open order across the fields. There were a few shops; we stopped to inquire. We were told that some of the prisoners had a couple of SS men cornered in there. We drove on, reached the main gate. The prisoners crowded up behind the wire. We entered.

And now, let me tell you this in the first person, for I was the least important person there, as you shall hear. There surged around me an evil-smelling horde. Men and boys reached out to touch me; they were in rags and the remnants of uniform. Death had already marked many of them, but they were smiling with their eyes. I looked out over that mass of men to the green fields beyond where well-fed Germans were plowing.

A German, Fritz Kersheimer, came up and said, "May I show you around the camp? I've been here ten years." An Englishman stood to attention, saying, "May I introduce myself, delighted to see you, and can you tell me when some of our blokes will be along?" I told him soon and asked to see one of the barracks. It happened to be occupied by

Czechoslovakians. When I entered, men crowded around, tried to lift me to their shoulders. They were too weak. Many of them could not get out of bed. I was told that this building had once stabled eighty horses. There were twelve hundred men in it, five to a bunk. The stink was beyond all description.

When I reached the center of the barracks, a man came up and said, "You remember me. I'm Peter Zenkl, one-time mayor of Prague." I remembered him, but did not recognize him. He asked about Benes and Jan Masaryk. I asked how many men had died in that building during the last month. They called the doctor; we inspected his records. There were only names in the little black book, nothing more — nothing of who these men were, what they had done, or hoped. Behind the names of those who had died was a cross. I counted them. They totaled 242. Two hundred and forty-two out of twelve hundred in one month.

As I walked down to the end of the barracks, there was applause from the men too weak to get out of bed. It sounded like the hand clapping of babies; they were so weak. The doctor's name was Paul Heller. He had been there since 1938.

As we walked out into the courtyard, a man fell dead. Two others — they must have been over sixty — were crawling toward the latrine. I saw it but will not describe it.

In another part of the camp they showed me the children, hundreds of them. Some were only six. One rolled up his sleeve, showed me his number. It was tattooed on his arm. D-6030, it was. The others showed me their numbers; they will carry them until they die.

An elderly man standing next to me said, "The children, enemies of the state." I could see their ribs through their thin shirts. The old man said, "I am Professor Charles Richer of the Sorbonne." The children clung to my hands and stared. We crossed to the courtyard. Men kept coming up to speak to me and to touch me, professors from Poland, doctors from Vienna, men from all of Europe. Men from the countries that made America.

We went to the hospital; it was full. The doctor told me that two hundred had died the day before. I asked the cause of death; he shrugged and said,

"Tuberculosis, starvation, fatigue, and there are many who have no desire to live. It is very difficult." Dr. Heller pulled back the blankets from a man's feet to show me how swollen they were. The man was dead. Most of the patients could not move.

As we left the hospital I drew out a leather billfold, hoping that I had some money which would help those who lived to get home. Professor Richer from the Sorbonne said, "I should be careful of my wallet if I were you. You know there are criminals in this camp, too." A small man tottered up, saying, "May I feel the leather, please? You see, I used to make good things of leather in Vienna." Another man said, "My name is Walter Roeder. For many years I lived in Joliet. Came back to Germany for a visit and Hitler grabbed me."

I asked to see the kitchen; it was clean. The German in charge had been a Communist, had been at Buchenwald for nine years, had a picture of his daughter in Hamburg. He hadn't seen her in twelve years, and if I got to Hamburg, would I look her up? He showed me the daily ration — one piece of brown bread about as thick as your thumb, on top of it a piece of margarine as big as three sticks of chewing gum. That, and a little stew, was what they received every twenty-four hours. He had a chart on the wall; very complicated it was. There were little red tabs scattered through it. He said that was to indicate each ten men who died. He had to account for the rations, and he added, "We're very efficient here."

We went again into the courtyard, and as we walked, we talked. The two doctors, the Frenchman and the Czech, agreed that about six thousand had died during March. Kersheimer, the German, added that back in the winter of 1939, when the Poles began to arrive without winter clothing, they died at the rate of approximately nine hundred a day. Five different men asserted that Buchenwald was the best concentration camp in Germany; they had had some experience of the others.

Dr. Heller, the Czech, asked if I would care to see the crematorium. He said it wouldn't be very interesting because the Germans had run out of coke some days ago and had taken to dumping the bodies into a great hole nearby. Professor Richer said perhaps I would care to see the small courtyard. I said yes. He turned and told the children to stay behind. As we walked across the square I noticed that the professor had a hole in his left shoe and a toe sticking out of the right one. He followed my eyes and said, "I regret that I am so little presentable, but what can one do?" At that point, another Frenchman came up to announce that three of his fellow countrymen outside had killed three SS men and taken one prisoner. We proceeded to the small courtyard. The wall was about eight feet high; it adjoined what had been a stable or a garage. We entered. It was floored with concrete. There were two rows of bodies stacked up like cordwood. They were thin and very white. Some of the bodies were terribly bruised, though there seemed to be little flesh to bruise. Some had been shot through the head, but they bled but little. All except two were naked. I tried to count them as best as I could and arrived at the conclusion that all that was mortal of more than five hundred men and boys lay there in two neat piles.

There was a German trailer which must have contained another fifty, but it wasn't possible to count them. The clothing was piled in a heap against the wall. It appeared that most of the men and boys had died of starvation; they had not been executed. But the manner of death seemed unimportant. Murder had been done at Buchenwald. God alone knows how many men and boys have died there during the last twelve years. Thursday I was told that there were more than twenty thousand in the camp. There had been as many as sixty thousand. Where are they now? As I left that camp, a Frenchman who used to work for Havas in Paris came up to me and said, "You will write something about this, perhaps?" And he added, "To write about this you must have been here at least two years, and after that — you don't want to write anymore."

I pray you to believe what I have said about Buchenwald. I have reported what I saw and heard, but only part of it. For most of it I have no words. Dead men are plentiful in war, but the living dead, more than twenty thousand of them in one camp. And the country round about was pleasing to the eye, and the Germans were well fed and well dressed. American trucks were rolling to the rear, filled with prisoners. Soon they would be eating American rations, as much for a meal as the men at Buchenwald received in four days.

If I've offended you by this rather mild account of Buchenwald, I'm not in the least bit sorry. I was there on Thursday, and many men in many tongues blessed the name of Roosevelt. For long years his name has meant the full measure of their hope. These men who had kept close company with death for many years did not know that Mr. Roosevelt would, within hours, join their comrades who had laid their lives on the scales of freedom.

Back in 1941, Mr. Churchill said to me with tears in his eyes, "One day the world and history will recognize and acknowledge what it owes your president." I saw and heard the first installment of that at Buchenwald on Thursday. It came from all over Europe. Their faces, with more flesh on them, might have been found anywhere at home. To them the name "Roosevelt" was a symbol, the code word for a lot of guys named "Joe" who are somewhere out in the blue with the armor heading east. At Buchenwald, they spoke of the president just before he died. If there be a better epitaph, history does not record it.

Murrow, who twenty years earlier re-
proached European students for their hos-
tility to Germans, now shared those feelings. Dick Hottelet, a former prisoner of
the Gestapo, told Ed he should be
ashamed of himself. Ed might have been
feeling guilty, too. He could not have
looked upon the dead and dying of
Buchenwald without thinking of the thousands he could not help through the
Emergency Committee in the 1930s.
Never mind that without his help hundreds more would have shared the fate
of Buchenwald's victims, Ed had seen the
price of failure.

Even his V-E Day broadcast was a sober
reflection on the cost of war. Although he
reported on the victory hoopla in Pic-
cadilly Circus, he also observed that "some
people appear not to be part of the cele-
bration. Their minds must be filled with
the memories of friends who died in the
streets where they now walk." Likewise,
when the Japanese surrendered and the
long war was finally over, Ed's focus was on
the new challenges posed to a world that
now had nuclear weapons.

Personally and professionally, Ed Murrow should have been on top of the world in 1945. He had survived the war and enjoyed the highest reputation for his journalism. He and the people he hired had transformed the medium of radio. Although his health was not the best, he was still just thirty-seven years old and had the option to continue broadcasting, write books, become a college president, foundation director, or corporate executive. Best of all, he was now a father with the birth of his son Casey on November 6.

Bill Paley wanted Ed back in New York, running the news operations of CBS. Ed's decision to take the job was not an easy one, for it meant turning down an attractive offer from Campbell's Soup to sponsor a daily Murrow news program. One motivation for taking the executive job was to keep the Murrow Boys on the team. Jobs in print journalism still paid more money in 1945, and the CBS reporters were getting offers. Bill Paley's flattery certainly was a factor, and so was the opportunity to shape policy at CBS.

During Christmas week, CBS announced that Ed Murrow would be its new vice president and director of public affairs. Paley was moving up to chairman. The ailing Paul Kesten would be replaced by his prótége, Frank Stanton, who was named president. In March, Ed made his last broadcast from London, and the BBC engineers presented him with the microphone he had used there so often. It now had an inscription:

This microphone, taken from Studio B4
of Broadcasting House, London, is
presented to
EDWARD R. MURROW
who used it there with such distinction for
so many broadcasts to CBS New York
during the war years 1939 to 1945
March 8th 1946

Ed left the London bureau in the hands of Howard K. Smith and booked passage home. He and Janet returned to the country where they'd had no home since 1937. They were parents now. Murrow, a fearless reporter, was now vice president of a high-profile New York corporation. Adjustments would have to be made. Or not.

7

Transition

Murrow began his CBS career as Paul White's equal, became White's underling with the move to Europe, and returned to New York as White's boss. The old rivalry was over, and White had lost. The two could not share the same newsroom for long, and they didn't. White's drinking, an office embarrassment, increased, and his ability to function was further diminished by the pain-killers he took for arthritis.

In the spring of 1946, CBS Radio began its new nightly roundup, sponsored by Campbell's Soup, with Robert Trout in the role the soup company had offered Murrow. Paul White insisted on introducing the program, and calmed his mike fright by making several trips to a neighborhood tavern. By airtime, White was sloshed, and every listener could tell. CBS announced his resignation days later.

As the new vice president and director

of public affairs, Ed established a documentary unit and introduced several new programs. *You Are There*, originally *CBS Is There*, employed actors playing historical figures being "interviewed" by CBS. *As Others See Us* was a review of foreign press coverage of the United States. *CBS Views the Press* was a pet project for Murrow. Hosted by Don Hollenbeck, the program examined the performance of print journalism.

New reporters hired by Murrow included Paris correspondent David Schoenbrun, a former teacher who worked in army intelligence during the war. Covering Vienna was East European expert Alexander Kendrick, later Murrow's first biographer. The new Middle East reporter was a young decorated war veteran, George Polk. The next group of hires included Daniel Schorr, Robert Pierpoint, and others who went on to serve CBS for decades.

Not all reporters were equal. The original Murrow Boys, the wartime reporting crew, had a swagger about them. They were the favorite sons, and they relished their status. Others on the news staff resented the Boys' status and formed the Murrow Is Not God Club, offering membership to Janet. The club lost some of its effectiveness when Murrow heard about it and applied for membership.

Paley believed Murrow was a good manager — firm but fair, and pragmatic when necessary. Murrow seemed to know which staff members were better motivated by a pat on the back and which by a swift kick in the tail. Neither method worked with the first man he had hired, once his closest friend. William L. Shirer was Ed's biggest personnel failure.

Shirer had a Sunday program of news and analysis sponsored by the J. B. Williams Company, makers of shaving products. His ratings had fallen, and Williams decided to drop its sponsorship. Accounts differ as to whether Shirer learned the news from his agent, from the sponsor, from Murrow, or accidentally from someone at Williams's advertising agency. Ed offered Shirer another time slot without a sponsor, but there was a substantial difference in income between a sponsored and an unsponsored program.

On March 23, Shirer concluded his broadcast by saying the following Sunday's program would be his last. Then he told waiting reporters (although he denied calling a news conference) that he was being gagged because of his liberal views. Liberal activists took their cue and picketed the CBS building at 485 Madison Avenue in New York. Stung by Shirer's charge, Ed announced that Shirer's time slot would go to Joseph C. Harsch of the *Christian Science Monitor* and that this would "improve Columbia's news analysis in this period." Now both Shirer and Murrow deliberately had said something hurtful toward the other.

Just nine years earlier, the two men had pioneered overseas broadcast journalism in covering Hitler's annexation of Austria. They had been to each other the best friend either of them ever had. The disintegration of their friendship might have begun when Shirer left Europe at the end of 1940, returning to the United States to write, lecture, and have a CBS program out of New York. To Murrow, it had reeked of "cashing in" on their war coverage. For his part, Shirer believed Murrow was jealous because Shirer's *Berlin Diary* had outsold Murrow's *This Is London*. Now, in 1947, Murrow believed that Shirer had grown lazy and was not doing enough legwork for his broadcasts. Smith, Sevareid, and other colleagues also believed Shirer had been "coasting" on his wartime reputation.

Shirer and Murrow tried to patch it up and presented Paley with a written agreement of the conditions under which Shirer would continue with CBS. Paley, however, rejected the agreement; the incident had embarrassed CBS and soured him on Shirer. Murrow did not press the matter, and Shirer was through at Columbia. Shirer was heard on the Mutual Broadcasting System for a couple of years, then left radio to write books, including *Stranger Come Home*, a roman à clef about a reporter, a network executive, and a demagogic U.S. senator. His *Rise and Fall of the Third Reich* became a publishing phenomenon in 1959, followed by multiple volumes of well-received memoirs. Although Shirer and Murrow would have further contact, Shirer went to his grave believing Murrow had sabotaged the broadcasting career of William L. Shirer.

This was the nadir of Ed's brief executive career and added to his frustration at being unable to establish a clear editorial policy at CBS. He had drafted a report that was to acknowledge that absolute objectivity was nearly impossible but that CBS would have fairness as its goal and be generous with airtime for multiple points of view on controversial issues. Before Ed could issue the report, the FCC announced plans to revisit the issue of advocacy in broadcasting. In the Cold War atmosphere of 1947, when people feared Communist infiltration of every U.S. institution, the FCC announcement was a warning that broadcasters had best be careful not to stray far from Establishment views. Murrow's editorial policy was filed away forever.

Ed's resignation from management was announced on July 19, 1947. He and Paley had mutually concluded that Ed was happier on the air than he was in the executive suite. Among the *un*happy was Eric Sevareid, who had taken the job of Washington bureau chief on the assurance that Ed would be his insulation from intrusion by top management.

Another man upset was Robert Trout, a major CBS personality since before Murrow joined the network. Trout was a tall, dapper gentleman with a mustache that made him look like one of those British swells from a 1930s movie inviting you to "summer" with him in Switzerland. After long and loyal service to CBS, he'd finally been allowed to take his star turn. He'd been the voice of *The News 'Til Now*, enjoying the perks that went with fronting the network's premier evening news roundup. Although he had more than eight years left on a ten-year contract, Trout was bumped from his program. *The News 'Til Now* was becoming *Edward R. Murrow with the News*. Trout left the network for NBC but would return a few years later.

Murrow launched his fifteen-minute program at 7:45 P.M. on September 29, 1947. It ran for twelve years and was the most authoritative news broadcast on radio. Jesse Zousmer and later Ed Bliss wrote the hard news. Johnny Aaron handled the "word of the day" feature. Murrow dictated his closing commentary to his personal assistant, Kay Campbell, who'd been brought over from the London bureau. Later, Ed hired Raymond Gram Swing to do some of his writing. After the nightly broadcast, the men unwound at Colbee's Bar and Grill near the CBS offices on Madison Avenue.

There was no dearth of news to report. The Marshall Plan, although one of the finest moments of American generosity, angered the Soviets, who warned East European governments that they were to refuse aid from Washington. East and West were growing more apart. Americans feared communism, and U.S. politicians exploited that fear.

On October 27, 1947, Ed's broadcast addressed the House Un-American Activities Committee hearings on alleged Communists in Hollywood, declaring that Congress usually investigated "what individuals . . . have or have not done, rather than what individuals think." Murrow said, "The right of dissent — or, if you prefer, the right to be wrong — is surely fundamental to the existence of a democratic society. That's the right that went first in every nation that stumbled down the trail of totalitarianism." He ended by quoting Adolf Hitler: "The great strength of the totalitarian state is that it will force those who fear it to imitate it."

In 1948 Ed lost three good friends to the Cold War. When Communists took over the government of Czechoslovakia in March, Foreign Minister Jan Masaryk was found dead on the ground below his third-floor apartment. The Communists said Masaryk jumped, but Ed believed a man committing suicide picks a higher spot than the third floor. In May, CBS correspondent George Polk was murdered while covering a Communist insurgency in Greece. Then in December, the body of Laurence

Duggan was found on the sidewalk sixteen floors below the New York office of the Institute of International Education, which he served as director, having succeeded his father, Stephen, Ed's mentor at the IIE.

Ed's grief over Duggan's death turned to fury when Karl Mundt and Richard Nixon of the House Un-American Activities Committee said that Duggan had been identified as a Communist who had passed papers between ex-Communist Whittaker Chambers and ex-State Department official Alger Hiss. Ed went on the air with testimonials to Duggan's character from senior Washington officials, then concluded, "The members of the committee who have done this thing . . . may now consult their actions and their consciences."

Ed was outraged that Mundt and Nixon didn't have to offer proof of their accusation against a dead man. In the political climate of the time, proof wasn't necessary. Proof would come, however, long after Murrow's death. When the Soviet Union collapsed in 1991, files in Moscow were opened to some Western investigators. According to those who say they've seen those files, Laurence Duggan was a KGB informer.

Some columnists and broadcasters proclaimed their opposition to communism, but Murrow simply continued to report the news. The FBI, under J. Edgar Hoover, began a file on Murrow at about the same time that Secretary of Defense James Forrestal tried to recruit the broadcaster for the government. Such was the division in Washington over Ed Murrow; he was useful to Hoover as a potential scalp, but useful to Forrestal as a shaper of policy. Ed took neither Hoover's bait nor Forrestal's job.

Both CBS and NBC began broadcasting nightly news on television in 1948. The veteran correspondents of both networks wanted nothing to do with the new medium. The advertising dollars and the audience still belonged to radio. No one yet was called an "anchorman" in 1948, but Douglas Edwards was persuaded to be the first to assume that role for CBS-TV. His producer was a young man named Don Hewitt, later the creator of *60 Minutes.*

The 1948 national political conventions were the first to be televised, and Ed Murrow was a floor reporter, weighed down by many pounds of electronic gear as he attempted to interview delegates. The Murrows now owned a nice farm in Pawling, New York, a predominantly Republican community. Indeed, the Republican nominee lived there, too. Janet Murrow said the ladies of Pawling were choosing their gowns for the balls they'd attend at Thomas E. Dewey's inauguration until election day in November, when they heard the news of President Harry Truman's upset victory. Ed Murrow liked Dewey but was delighted that the pollsters had been proven so wrong.

Ed had a better year in 1949, winning the duPont-Columbia, Headliner, and Overseas Press Club awards while also being elected to the board of directors of CBS.

Some good ideas of 1949 were developed into Murrow radio programs. *This I Believe* was a series in which successful people, introduced by Murrow, would state their personal philosophies. Eleanor Roosevelt, Thomas Mann, Margaret Mead, Ralph Bunche, and Helen Hayes were among those on the program. Produced by Edward P. Morgan and later by Raymond Gram Swing, *This I Believe* also was broadcast by the Voice of America and syndicated in eighty-five newspapers. Texts of the personal philosophies were anthologized in two books that sold well. Also in 1949, CBS began its year-end tradition of having its farflung correspondents gather in

New York with Murrow for a discussion of the world situation. Called *Years of Crisis*, it might have been the ultimate "talking heads" program, but critics liked it. It was also important to the newer correspondents, for to be invited was a sign of arrival at Ed's inner circle.

Unfortunately, 1949 was also the year that the Soviet Union successfully tested its first nuclear weapons and when Communists took control in China. American politicians used these developments to their advantage, creating fear and hysteria and giving the cause of anticommunism a new urgency. Republicans, who had not elected a president since 1932, needed issues, and "Who leaked the bomb secrets?" and "Who lost China?" fit the bill. There *must* have been traitors in the Roosevelt and Truman administrations.

Spearheading the hunt for government Reds was Republican senator Joseph McCarthy, an ambitious fellow who, lacking any positive vision that captured the public's imagination, found his opportunity in bullying. He made charges against both well-known policymakers and unknown clerks. Murrow conceded that there might indeed be Communists or ex-Communists in Washington, but those accused should have the protections of the Bill of Rights. He also pointed out to his listeners that McCarthy offered no proof to back up his accusations.

Letters of outrage at Murrow's broadcasts piled up at the headquarters of Campbell's Soup. Whether McCarthy or Murrow was right didn't matter; controversy was not good for selling soup. The company told him it would no longer sponsor his news program after June 1950. This did not have an adverse effect on CBS because the network brought in more money by selling the program to regional sponsors. Eric Sevareid was not so lucky; he lost two sponsored programs after broadcasts critical of McCarthy.

Red-baiting reached right into CBS itself that June with the publication of *Red Channels*, a book that listed 151 names of broadcasting figures who had suspect "affiliations." The book was published by American Business Consultants, Inc., a firm begun by three former FBI agents who charged companies money to have their employees "cleared," or found to be without taint of communism. Big money was to be made in the blacklisting business, and American Business Consultants made a bunch of it by putting out mail-order bulletins under the name *Counterattack: The Newsletter of Facts about Communism*. A number of CBS employees were listed in *Red Channels*, including two of Murrow's correspondents, Howard K. Smith and Alexander Kendrick. Neither lost his job at CBS. Others did, however, and CBS ultimately skipped the middleman and did its own Red-hunting, assigning company attorney Daniel O'Shea as in-house "clearer" of present and prospective employees. All CBS employees were required to sign a loyalty oath. Many at CBS looked to Murrow to lead a backlash against the oath and refuse to sign, but Murrow replied, "I'll sign it and so will you." Ed picked his battles carefully. His stand for the Constitution was just ahead.

The Red scare affected government policy, domestic and foreign. No one's loyalty was assumed. Public figures felt it necessary to declare their allegiance to flag, country, and anticommunism. The Truman administration actively supported the French battle against Ho Chi Minh's forces in Vietnam. Then, after just five years of peace, Truman sent U.S. soldiers back to war, in Korea.

Arriving in Tokyo, where General Douglas MacArthur had his headquarters,

Ed was met by Bill Downs, who told him, "Go back, this ain't our kind of war." Journalists covering the Korean War questioned MacArthur's tactics as being pointless and risky. MacArthur responded by expelling reporters or by pressuring news organizations to recall correspondents who had offended him. Some journalists who questioned U.S. involvement in a civil war among Koreans found that doubts were raised about their loyalty. The Red scare was having a chilling effect on war reporting. A Murrow report challenging the military's assessment of the war was killed by the top brass of CBS. Ed was censored by his own network on his own program. At a luncheon in New York, Bill Paley told CBS correspondents to be careful of what they said in their broadcasts in these difficult times. Paley's directive reflected how CBS had changed. It was now a publicly held corporation diversifying into other interests besides broadcasting, and Paley was responsible to stockholders. Politicians had ways of dealing with a corporation like CBS, and not just through the Federal Communications Commission. Paley and Murrow were close personal friends, but Ed must not become bad for business.

8
McCarthy

Ferdinand Friendly Wachenheimer merci-
fully was renamed Fred Friendly by his station manager at WEAN in Providence,
Rhode Island. That was when he was a
radio producer before the war. He was still
interested in sound recordings in 1947,
when he pitched an idea to an agent, J. G.
Gude. Friendly proposed making a set of
phonograph records using the voices of
Churchill, Roosevelt, and other figures
prominent during the Great Depression and
World War II. The project needed a good
narrator, and Gude recommended his
client Edward R. Murrow. That was how
Murrow met Friendly, beginning one of the
most important and productive partnerships
in the history of broadcast journalism.

The record set, titled *I Can Hear It
Now*, 1933–45, was such a hit that Murrow
and Friendly collaborated on two more recordings. In 1950 Friendly joined CBS to

produce with Murrow a weekly radio newsmagazine series called *Hear It Now.* The program ran for six months beginning in December and included other contributors, such as CBS sports director Red Barber, the first man Ed hired back in his executive days. *Hear It Now* won a Peabody Award.

The third Murrow/Friendly project was, as Ed said on the first broadcast of *See It Now,* "an old team trying to learn a new trade." Radio veterans Murrow, Friendly, and CBS reporters Ed Scott and Joe Wershba had valuable help in learning how to work with pictures. The new team included independent producer Palmer Williams, film editor Mili Lerner Bonsignori, veteran newsreel cameramen Charlie Mack, Leo Rossi, Marty Barnett, and as studio director for the live Sunday telecasts, Don Hewitt, still spending weekdays as producer/director of *The CBS Evening News with Douglas Edwards.* Friendly proved to be a quick study, a little too quick perhaps for Hewitt, who observed, "Before I knew it, Friendly had replaced me at the head of the class."

See It Now premiered on November 18, 1951, and made a show of television itself. There was no studio set; Ed was seated in the control room of Studio 41 surrounded by the tools of the young medium: cameras, monitors, and the control panel, where Hewitt sat. The premiere began with a gimmick that would have been impossible with the technology in place just a month earlier. On Ed's cue, Hewitt called for a live shot of New York Harbor, which appeared on one of the monitors. On the adjacent monitor was a live shot of the Golden Gate Bridge in San Francisco. Two great American ports, three thousand miles apart, seen live simultaneously. The program also took viewers to London, Paris, Washington, and Korea.

Before *See It Now*, news on television was little more than the reading of headlines. The nightly news programs were only fifteen minutes long. Visuals were primitive; film took days and sometimes weeks to reach New York from abroad. On the *CBS Evening News*, Douglas Edwards occasionally referred to a filmed event as occurring "recently." *See It Now* had substance, the first program dealing with Korea, disarmament, a Churchill speech, and politics. It represented TV's arrival as a news medium and indicated potential for better things to come. Critics raved. One wrote, "It's been a long time a-comin', but we're beginning to See It Now." Finally, educated people would admit without shame that they owned a TV set.

For the second time, Edward R. Murrow had introduced a broadcasting medium to in-depth news. He was a pioneer of radio journalism in 1938 and television news in 1951. Techniques he introduced on both are still in use today, from the multipoint radio roundup to the split-screen TV interview. On both radio and TV he set a high standard for quality, for substance over froth. To both he brought the conscience of a serious journalist and the presence of a born broadcaster.

As in any good partnership, Murrow and Friendly complemented and completed each other. Ed gave the program its class and respectability. Friendly was the tyrant who drove the staff to get the job done. Friendly was a six-foot-four bear of a man with a booming voice and a short temper. He demanded perfection, and he threw pencils at staff members who didn't deliver. He'd say, "Ed would like . . ." or "Ed thinks we should . . . ," but the staff knew Friendly was speaking for himself.

Half an hour of programming each week doesn't sound like much, but given the sweeping ambition of what *See It Now* tried to accomplish with 1951's technology, it's a wonder anyone on staff stayed with the program for long. Excellence was demanded and expected; only 5 percent of the film shot was used; the rest fell to the cutting room floor. That might have been unacceptable for another program, but *See It Now* was a fiefdom that never came under the supervision of Sig Mickelson, the man in charge of TV news at CBS.

See It Now was just a month old when it first addressed Senator Joseph McCarthy, showing him whining about being "kicked around and bullwhipped" by his critics. That film was followed by other film showing McCarthy in his customary role as the one doing the kicking and the bullwhipping. Despite this early example of what TV was capable of doing, the program received little attention from viewers. The medium was still new and audiences were small, especially on Sunday afternoons.

Early in 1952, *See It Now*, already the winner of a Peabody and the first George Polk Award, had its second broadcast about McCarthy. Interviewed live for three minutes, McCarthy ignored Ed's questions about the rights of the accused and instead hammered Senator William

Benton of Connecticut, who was trying to get McCarthy expelled from the Senate. McCarthy called Benton a mental midget hiding behind congressional immunity. A week later on *See It Now*, Murrow used a transcript to illustrate McCarthy's lies, then interviewed Benton about McCarthy's tactics.

The presidential election was a frequent program topic that year. Sig Mickelson asked Murrow to be the principal correspondent for CBS coverage of the political party national conventions. When Ed said no, Mickelson chose a new CBS personality, who had picked up TV experience at WTOP in Washington, D.C. Walter Cronkite was a TV natural who won the convention ratings derby for CBS. It was at these 1952 conventions that CBS first used the term "anchorman," for which both Mickelson and Don Hewitt claimed credit. Although he had urged CBS to hire Cronkite, Ed Murrow had not forgiven him for turning down an offer to join Murrow's Boys in 1943. On the air, Murrow treated Cronkite with collegiality, but off the air, with condescension.

Dwight Eisenhower was elected president and made good on his campaign pledge to go to Korea. Murrow and a small army from CBS went there, too, for a *See It Now* one-hour special called "Christmas in Korea," hailed by the *New York Times* as "a masterpiece of reportorial artistry." *Variety* noted that what Eisenhower saw on his trip was still a secret but "What Murrow & Co. saw, the American people saw."

On the way home, Ed was hospitalized in Renton, Washington, for flu and exhaustion. A few weeks later, he checked into another hospital for a week of tests that proved negative.

On Friday, October 2, 1953, Ed launched another weekly program. *Person to Person*, the brainchild of Ed's radio writers Johnny Aaron and Jesse Zousmer, was a CBS "visit" to the homes of celebrities such as actress Mary Martin, baseball player Roy Campanella, Senator John F. Kennedy, and comedian Sid Caesar. The celebrity showed a camera crew around the house while talking with Ed, who remained at a CBS studio. It was pure fluff; rarely was anything of substance discussed. To his credit, Ed wanted some programs to deal with average people, but viewers wrote to say they wanted to see the "beautiful people." The television ancestor of the Barbara Walters star schmooze, *Person to Person* was an instant ratings hit. Murrow's friends and associates were aghast that he was taking part in something totally out of character for him, asking him why he would stoop to do *that* show. Sometimes he said he did it as a favor to longtime associates Aaron and Zousmer. On other occasions he spoke of the goodwill it gave him with CBS, delivering a hit show to an employer that might now be more tolerant of *See It Now*. He also hoped his exposure on *Person to Person* might deliver a bigger audience to *See It Now*. It didn't hurt that Ed owned a big chunk of *Person to Person* and became a moderately rich man when he bought Zousmer and Aaron's shares and eventually sold the show to Paley and CBS.

Don Hewitt said critic John Horne of the *New York Herald Tribune* coined the terms "high Murrow" for *See It Now* and "low Murrow" for *Person to Person*. The contrast could not have been marked better than it was that October. Just days after the premiere of the breezy *Person to Person*, the substantive *See It Now* returned to the subject of McCarthyism.

Ed found the story of Milo Radulovich in the *Detroit News*. Having served eight years in the air force, the twenty-six-year-old Lieutenant Radulovich was to be severed from the reserves because he had "close associations" with the wrong people, namely his father and his sister. Radulovich's sister was suspected of being a Communist sympathizer for having walked a picket line. The father's big crime was his subscription to a Serbian-language newspaper. Serbia was then part of Yugoslavia, which was no longer allied with Moscow when the Radulovich case arose.

One could not determine if the charges against the Radulovich family were any more serious than that because the lieutenant was not allowed to know the specific charges contained in an envelope that was never opened at his hearing. The air force also did not say where the allegations came from, nor did it call any witnesses. Whatever the charges, they had nothing to do with Radulovich himself. All he had to do to retain his commission was to denounce his family. On *See It Now* Radulovich asked rhetorically, "If I am being judged by my relatives, are my children going to be asked to denounce me?"

Murrow's closing remarks moved the program from exposé to editorial:

We believe that the son shall not bear the iniquity of the father, even though that iniquity be proved; and in this case it was not. . . . Whatever happens in the whole area of the relationship between the individual and the state, we do it ourselves . . . it seems to Fred Friendly and myself . . . that this is a subject that should be argued about endlessly.

In the *New York Times*, critic Jack Gould observed it was the first time that a network and sponsor had consented to "a vigorous editorial." Consent yes, in the sense that they didn't kill the program before it was broadcast, but CBS did not promote *See It Now* that week. Murrow and Friendly spent $1,500 of their own money to buy an ad promoting the program in the *New York Times*.

Five weeks after the Radulovich program, the air force announced that it had concluded that the lieutenant's family did not pose a grave security risk and that the lieutenant would retain his commission. There is no question that this development resulted from Ed's broadcast.

Senator Joseph McCarthy understood that the Radulovich program was really about him. The following month, McCarthy's investigator Donald Surine buttonholed *See It Now* reporter Joe Wershba at a hearing on Capitol Hill. Surine handed Wershba a photostat of a 1935 story from the *Sun-Telegraph*, then a Hearst paper in Pittsburgh. The story was about the exchange program Murrow had fostered while working for the Institute of International Education. The story suggested that the Soviet Union was training Americans to teach in American schools. In his remarks to Wershba, Surine made it clear that republication of the charge would be the price of Murrow's further pursuit of McCarthy.

McCarthy's threat backfired. When Wershba delivered the material to Murrow, Ed's response was to direct the staff to begin collecting archival film on the senator and to start filming all of his speeches and congressional hearings. The very next *See It Now* program served as a sort of Murrow response to McCarthy. "An Argument in Indianapolis" concerned an attempt by the American Civil Liberties Union to hold a meeting in the Hoosier capital. The ACLU was unable to find a venue for its meeting because of pressure by the American Legion. Finally, a Catholic priest offered his parish hall. *See It Now* filmed the ACLU meeting and a simultaneous American Legion meeting held in protest just blocks away.

As *See It Now* prepared for its show-down with McCarthy, it continued doing programs inspired by McCarthyism. There was a program about Harry Dexter White, a Treasury Department official in the Truman administration. Eisenhower's attorney general, Herbert Brownell, charged that Truman had promoted White despite being told that White was a Soviet spy. Wiretaps, Fifth Amendment rights, and congressional investigations also were *See It Now* topics that season.

A Gallup poll taken in February 1954 showed a 50 percent approval rating for McCarthy despite his growing confrontation with the Eisenhower administration over investigations of "Communists" in the U.S. Army. That's when Murrow and Friendly decided the time was right for their McCarthy broadcast.

The *See It Now* staff was unusually tense at a film editing session on Sunday, March 7. They knew that their names on the credits of that week's program might mark them for investigation by McCarthy. Friendly asked if anyone on the staff had anything to hide. Murrow remarked, "The terror is right here in this room."

On Tuesday morning, the day of the

broadcast, Bill Paley told Murrow that he was with him that day and he'd be with him the next day, too. Promoting the program might have been a more obvious display of support, but that did not happen; once again, Murrow and Friendly paid for an ad in the *New York Times.*

Seconds before airtime, Friendly observed, "This is going to be a tough one." Murrow replied, "After this one, they're all going to be tough."

Murrow began by telling viewers that the entire program would be about McCarthy and that the senator could have equal time if he wanted it. Paley said he suggested Murrow make the offer right away, to beat McCarthy to the punch. The bulk of the program consisted of McCarthy on film giving speeches and conducting interrogations at hearings, with Murrow offering a point-by-point rebuttal. McCarthy claimed to advocate the two-party system, but Murrow reminded listeners that the senator had accused Democrats of treason. McCarthy held up secret documents, but Murrow said it was a hearing transcript available for two dollars. McCarthy said the ACLU was listed as a Communist front, but Murrow countered that the ACLU was on no government list of subversive groups and that it had received letters of commendation from Truman, Eisenhower, and General MacArthur. There were two speeches in which McCarthy was gloating over perceived triumphs, but these also worked against him because the gloat included a manic laugh that made him appear as some crazed fanatic. Film clips showing him badgering witnesses made him out as a bully. Adlai Stevenson, said McCarthy, was Alger Hiss's choice to attend a particular conference, but then Murrow named some Republicans who were there, too.

Then came the McCarthy-as-victim speech in which the senator protests "mud-slinging against the committee by the extreme left-wing elements of press and radio." At that point Murrow showed a tall stack of newspapers and said they were the papers opposed to McCarthy. Gesturing to a considerably shorter group of papers, Murrow said, "These are the ones that supported him." Murrow read from anti-McCarthy editorials, including some from the *Chicago Tribune* and the *New York Herald Tribune*, decidedly not left-wing papers.

McCarthy on film declared that he would carry the fight "regardless of who happens to be president" and quoted Shakespeare's line "Upon what meat does this our Caesar feed?" Murrow broke in with, "And upon what meat does Senator McCarthy feed? Two staples of his diet . . . the investigations, protected by immunity, and the half-truth." A bit later, Murrow said that had McCarthy looked three lines earlier in *Julius Caesar*, "he would have found this line, which is altogether not inappropriate: 'The fault, dear Brutus, is not in our stars, but in ourselves.' "

The broadcast was a devastating indictment of McCarthy and his methods, allowing the senator to hang himself with his own words and actions, then punctuated by Murrow's pointed rebuttal. There was a final knockout blow in Ed's closing commentary:

> No one familiar with the history of this country can deny that congressional committees are useful. It is necessary to investigate before legislating. But the line between investigation and persecuting is a very fine one, and the junior senator from Wisconsin has stepped over it repeatedly. His primary achievement has been in confusing the public mind between the internal and the ex-

ternal threat of Communism. We must not confuse dissent with disloyalty. We must remember always that accusation is not proof and that conviction depends upon evidence and due process of law. We will not walk in fear, one of another. We will not be driven by fear into an age of unreason if we dig deep in our history and our doctrine and remember that we are not descended from fearful men, not from men who feared to write, to speak, to associate, and to defend causes which were for the moment unpopular.

This is no time for men who oppose Senator McCarthy's methods to keep silent, *or* for those who approve. We can deny our heritage and our history, but we cannot escape responsibility for the result. As a nation we have come into our full inheritance at a tender age. We proclaim ourselves, as indeed we are, defenders of freedom — what's left of it — but we cannot defend freedom abroad by deserting it at home. The actions of the junior senator from Wisconsin have caused alarm and dismay amongst our allies abroad and given considerable aid and comfort to our enemies. And whose fault is that?

Not really his; he didn't create this situation of fear, he merely exploited it and rather successfully. Cassius was right. "The fault, dear Brutus, is not in our stars, but in ourselves." Good night, and good luck.

Public reaction ran overwhelmingly in Ed Murrow's favor, but a far more important result from the broadcast was the transformation of political discussion. The silent found their voice. The Eisenhower administration could counter McCarthy's hearings on the army knowing the senator's public support was fading.

The next *See It Now* featured McCarthy's investigation of Annie Lee Moss, allegedly a Communist spy who worked in the Pentagon's code room. Moss came across as an innocent, persecuted civil servant whom the committee may have confused with someone else of the same name. McCarthy left in the middle of Moss's appearance, suggesting he had retreated in embarrassment. Three years later, the Subversive Activities Control Board declared that Moss had, in fact, been a Communist in the 1940s. McCarthy's staff had found an actual Communist, and he still couldn't capitalize on it.

Murrow defended his program, saying the point was not Moss's politics but rather her right to due process.

McCarthy accepted the offer of equal time and wanted writer William F. Buckley Jr. to rebut Murrow. He was told "no substitutes." The senator then decided that Murrow's sponsor, ALCOA, should pay the production costs of the rebuttal filming. ALCOA passed the bill to CBS, and CBS paid it.

On April 5, the day before the broadcast of McCarthy's rebuttal, *See It Now*'s production manager, Palmer Williams, was told that for $100 he could get an audio copy of McCarthy's remarks. The tip came from someone at Hearst's Movietone News, supplier of *See It Now*'s cameramen, which shared a building with the lab processing the McCarthy film. Williams obtained the audio track and stenographers transcribed it, giving Murrow a text from which he could fashion a written rebuttal to the rebuttal. McCarthy looked awful in his broadcast, which did nothing to help his cause. When the senator finished, Ed held a press conference at the Commodore Hotel, where each reporter received a copy of Murrow's seven-page statement. A reporter asked how Ed could have a written statement if he had not seen the broadcast in advance. Ed replied, "Does Macy's tell Gimbel's?" The printed statement, which Murrow read aloud for reporters, ended with Murrow stating: "When the record is finally written, as it will be one day, it will answer the question who has helped the Communist cause and who has served his country better, Senator McCarthy or I? I would like to be remembered by the answer to that question."

The Army/McCarthy hearings were the senator's final undoing. The TV audience now evaluated his methods with a fresh perspective. The climax came when McCarthy went after a young lawyer who had nothing to do with the proceedings. Unfortunately for McCarthy, Joseph Welch of the same law firm was very much a part of the hearings, and he snapped at McCarthy, "Have you no shame? . . . Until this moment, Senator, I think I never gauged your cruelty or your recklessness. If it were in my power to forgive you for your reckless cruelty, I would do so. I like to think I'm a gentle man, but your forgiveness will have to come from someone other than me."

In December 1954 the Senate voted to censure McCarthy. He had begun the year with 50 percent of American public opinion behind him but ended the year unable to win backing from 50 percent of the Senate. Senator Joseph McCarthy was done, but McCarthy*ism* lived on.

Although 1954 was the year of McCarthy's downfall, it also was a year in which McCarthyism had profound consequences for Murrow and people close to him.

On the day after Ed's McCarthy broadcast, McCarthy's friend FBI director J. Edgar Hoover asked to see his agency's file on Edward R. Murrow. Dissatisfied with the results, he asked for more information. The Murrow file grew instantly.

In November, Ed was denied a renewal of his passport unless he signed an affidavit stating he'd never been a member of the Communist Party. He protested to passport officials in both New York and Washington. It would have taken years of legal action to make his civil rights point in court, and a reporter can't be without a passport for very long. He signed.

Just days after Murrow's decisive broadcast in March, Palmer Williams was summoned to the office of Daniel O'Shea, the in-house enforcer of the CBS blacklist. Williams's ex-wife had been a Communist and held Party meetings at their home.

O'Shea ordered Williams to sign his resignation. Williams was being treated worse than Milo Radulovich. Murrow and Friendly told Williams to sign nothing, and ultimately O'Shea backed down.

On March 9, Don Hollenbeck began his 11:00 P.M. newscast on the CBS affiliate in New York by saying he associated himself with everything Ed Murrow had just said about McCarthy. Hollenbeck had been a frequent Red-baiting target of Hearst newspaper columnist Jack O'Brien. Hollenbeck did not have the thick skin it took for Murrow and others to ignore the smear tactics. In June he killed himself. Murrow and Friendly decided to end their program's relationship with Hearst, the actual employer of *See It Now*'s camera crews. All were offered CBS employment, and all of them accepted.

Diligent Daniel O'Shea received an anonymous tip that Joe Wershba of Murrow's staff had belonged to leftist groups in the 1930s. Murrow and Friendly fought Wershba's firing for weeks. In July, Wershba let them off the hook and resigned.

The irony in CBS's angst over former lefties and alleged lefties was that management had known for years that a member of the news staff was an actual former Soviet spy. Winston Burdett had come clean when he had to sign his CBS loyalty oath in 1950, declaring he'd joined the Communist Party when he was a movie critic for the *Brooklyn Eagle* in the 1930s. It was the Party that sent Burdett to Europe in 1940, or he might never have become a foreign correspondent. CBS hired Burdett, first as a stringer, while he was in Finland gauging Finnish morale for the Soviet occupiers. For two years he juggled CBS and Soviet assignments in Stockholm, Moscow, Bucharest (where he met and married Lea Schiavi), Belgrade, Ankara, and Teheran. While he and Lea were working in Teheran, the Japanese attacked Pearl Harbor, and the United States entered the war. Burdett told his Soviet handlers that he was through with spying, through with the Soviets, and through with Communism. While he was away on a CBS assignment, Lea was murdered in Teheran. Burdett believed Italian Fascists were to blame. After the war, he learned she'd been assassinated on orders from Moscow.

Burdett became an anti-Communist and a friendly witness before a Senate panel in 1955. Burdett shocked his CBS colleagues by not only confessing his own past but also by providing names of other *Brooklyn Eagle* Communists of the 1930s. Some remained his friends; others believed him a traitor; still others regarded the informer as a rat. Murrow, who hired him, pleaded with the Boys for compassion. Winston Burdett remained with CBS, serving in semi-exile in Rome until the end of his career in 1978. No non-Italian knew more about his beat, and his reports from the Vatican sounded as beatific as any vision conjured up in the Holy City.

In the end, it was a CBS radio personality who killed the blacklist, at heavy personal cost, with help from Ed Murrow and Charles Collingwood. John Henry Faulk worked for WCBS, the CBS-owned station in New York, and in 1956 was becoming a popular guest on network radio and TV programs. Like other CBS employees whose voices were heard on the air, Faulk was a member of the American Federation of Television and Radio Artists (AFTRA), the union representing broadcast workers. Happy to show that a labor union could be just as "American" as the employers it was supposed to be challenging, AFTRA was at that time an active participant in blacklisting. Texas-born Johnny Faulk was no Communist, but he had certain notions about the First Amendment that rendered Redbaiters offensive to him. Faulk hatched a plan to take control of AFTRA's New York local, and end its participation in blacklisting. He recruited Collingwood to run for president of the New York local, with actor Orson Bean as a candidate for first vice president and Faulk as a candidate for second vice president. They called themselves the Middle of the Road Slate, opposed to both Communism and blacklisting. No sooner had they won than the Redbaiters moved on them. Collingwood was too big to be vulnerable, but not the others. Pressure from blacklisters forced Bean to resign from the local board, allowing his career to continue. Faulk resisted and paid for his principles. The sponsor of his radio program abandoned him, so ultimately WCBS dropped him, too. He found himself unhireable.

Faulk took his problem to Murrow. Ed gave him $7,500 to hire attorney Louis Nizer. Ed said it was not a loan, but an investment in America. The case dragged on for seven years, but thanks to testimony by Collingwood, producers David Susskind and Mark Goodson, actress Kim Hunter, and Garry Moore, another popular CBS personality of the era, Faulk prevailed. In 1962 a jury determined that the blacklisters owed damages to John Henry Faulk. Although a few performers were still unwelcome on the air, the blacklist was dead. Unfortunately, so were Don Hollenbeck and other victims of the anti-Communist hysteria. Some who'd fled the country could return, but many ruined careers could never be revived.

9
See It Not

The thanks *See It Now* received for doing the most significant program in broadcast journalism was to lose both its sponsor and its slot in prime time. A normal television program thrives on being the talk of car pools and coffee breaks, but a news program scores that kind of buzz only when it's controversial; television shunned controversy in the days when regulation was taken seriously.

ALCOA, makers of aluminum products, needed some respect and class when it agreed to sponsor *See It Now* in 1951, and it got that by being associated with Ed Murrow. But in the spring of 1954, ALCOA did not need to be linked to the guy who was fighting the guy who was fighting Communists. ALCOA long has been praised for sticking around for *See It Now*'s first three years, but what about the next four years? ALCOA announced the dropping of its sponsorship less than two months after the McCarthy broadcast and just days after a program about a small newspaper's story of a land scandal in Texas where ALCOA was expanding operations. Coincidence?

As for the exile from prime time, Murrow predicted that move in June when he glanced at a studio monitor and got his first look at *The $64,000 Question* and remarked, "Any bets on how long we'll keep this time period now?" *The $64,000 Question* spawned many imitators on CBS and the other networks. CBS could not afford to have the moneylosing *See It Now* occupying a time slot that could be given over to yet another moneymaking quiz program.

See It Now soldiered on back in the Sunday ghetto. Before it was done, *See It Now* carried programs on the Suez crisis, Communist Poland, anti-immigration protests in Delaware, two hours on cigarettes and health, book banning in California, *Brown v. Board of Education*, presidential succession, emerging African nations, automation, teenagers, Las Vegas, Cold War neutrality, the stock exchange, apartheid in South Africa, a college debate on recognizing China, and immigration policy. *See It Now* was a big "follower." It followed Margaret Chase Smith around the world, followed Marian Anderson on an Asian tour, followed the making of a Hollywood movie, and followed a single pint of blood from the arm of a donor in the United States to the arm of an American soldier in Korea.

See It Now flew through the eye of a hurricane, watched the Missouri River rise, and rode the *Orient Express.* There were Murrow interviews with the presidential candidates of 1952 and 1956, plus Carl Sandburg, Harry Truman, Harold Macmillan, Tito, Chou En-lai, Dr. Jonas Salk, George Marshall (the only general to win the Nobel Peace Prize), and Dr. Robert Oppenheimer. The Oppenheimer interview was controversial because the physicist had lost his security clearance. CBS blacklist commissar Daniel O'Shea was upset about it, but Bill Paley loved the program.

There were others Paley did not like, and these resulted in his offering free time to opponents of Murrow's and Friendly's broadcasts. One involved Senator John Bricker of Ohio, who opposed U.S. agreement to treaties on human rights, labor, and other social issues. Bricker sought to limit presidential treaty-making powers by requiring that treaties be approved by both houses of Congress and by state legislatures. Bricker was incensed that *See It Now* gave his position just eight minutes, fifty-three seconds of airtime, while opponents of his amendment were heard for eleven minutes, two seconds. A second program on the Bricker amendment failed to mollify the senator, whose stopwatch told him that collectively his side got a mere fourteen minutes, fifty-nine seconds, while opponents got a whopping fifteen minutes, fourteen seconds. Bricker must have blamed CBS for his amendment's one-vote loss in the Senate, for he introduced a bill that would have imposed direct FCC regulation of broadcast networks.

The Bricker threat illustrated the gap between Paley and Murrow. Paley believed Murrow's attitude of "just do the news and let the chips fall where they may" to be foolish and reckless. In those days, the FCC was not the feckless captive of the broadcasting industry, it was an agency with rules and regulations that it enforced on that industry. Paley's sensitivity to offending the likes of Bricker raised the question of whether it was possible for a regulated broadcaster to have any credibility as a news organization.

Balanced programs also got Murrow into trouble. The Suez broadcast was warmly received in Israel, but American Jews hated it. They were outraged that the Egyptian point of view was aired.

A *See It Now* program on the plight of the small farmer carried the equal-time question to ridiculous lengths. Secretary of Agriculture Ezra Taft Benson insisted the small farmer was not in trouble. He was given a rebuttal program, which he used to praise the Eisenhower administration's farm policy in an election year. This, in turn, upset the Democrats, two of whom were given a program to rebut the Benson program, which rebutted the original program, which was about the small farmer, who by now everyone had forgotten in the political back-and-forth.

The final *See It Now* battle over equal time was a program that shouldn't have been controversial at all, since it concerned the prospects for statehood for Alaska and Hawaii. On the program, union leader Harry Bridges called a congressman "crazy" for believing that Hawaii would be Communist-controlled. CBS, without consulting Murrow or Friendly, gave the congressman equal time so he could say that Hawaiian statehood was "a major objective of the Communist conspiracy."

Perhaps it was the tenor of such intellectual dialogue that made Murrow snap at CBS that he couldn't continue doing the program if the network was going to continue undermining it with generous offers of equal time. In effect, CBS responded that he shouldn't, and it canceled *See It Now*. The last program, on the reemergence of Germany, ran in July 1958. Paley told Murrow that he no longer wanted the stomachaches that he got when Murrow did controversial programs. Murrow told Paley that they went with the job.

The death of *See It Now* was devastating to Murrow. The program established TV news, showed what it could do, and required that competing networks come up with similar programs. The timing of the cancellation was unfortunate for CBS because important people were beginning to ask questions about all the quiz shows that had produced record profits for the networks. Something didn't smell right about them.

His relationship with Paley and CBS deteriorating, Ed Murrow had a magnificent opportunity to make a clean break and begin a new life. He was invited by New York's Democratic Party to run for the Senate. Paley was enthusiastic and urged him to do it. Harry Truman counseled

Ed that his choice was between being the junior senator from New York or being Edward R. Murrow, beloved broadcast journalist and hero to millions. Ed listened to Truman.

Ed had lost *See It Now*, but he still had *Person to Person* and the nightly radio broadcast. However, much more was going on in the fertile mind of Ed Murrow, and he hatched yet another idea. *Small World* was a global conversation among Murrow and three others over long-distance telephone lines. Each of the parties was filmed, and the four films were synchronized once they all reached CBS in New York. It had the look of today's satellite interviews, very impressive in those days before satellites. The first program featured India's prime minister Jawaharlal Nehru from New Delhi; former New York governor Thomas E. Dewey from Portland, Maine; and writer Aldous Huxley from Turin. Another program included journalist Malcolm Muggeridge, actress Lauren Bacall, and Eric Johnston, head of the Motion Picture Association of America. Music obviously dominated the conversation of conductor Thomas Beecham, singer Maria Callas, and comic pianist Victor Borge. Senator Everett Dirksen, poet Carl Sandburg, and author C. North-cote Parkinson discussed Lincoln. Although humor was the topic for writer James Thurber, playwright Noël Coward, and Irish actress Siobhan McKenna, there was humor of a different sort when writer Brendan Behan did the program while quite drunk, to the great amusement of comedian Jackie Gleason. *Small World* had a modest but devoted audience and was well received by critics.

Small World had its first broadcast on October 12, 1958. Just three days later, Murrow was in Chicago to address the annual convention of the Radio-Television News Directors Association (RTNDA). The speech he gave that night reflected his deep hurt over the cancellation of *See It Now*. It was an angry speech, a bomb dropped on the broadcasting industry, with fair warning in the opening line:

This just might do nobody any good. At the end of this discourse a few people may accuse this reporter of fouling his own comfortable nest, and your organization may be accused of giving hospitality to heretical and even dangerous thoughts. But the elaborate structure of networks, advertising agencies, and sponsors will not be shaken or altered. It is my desire, if not my duty, to try to talk to you journeymen with some candor about what is happening to radio and television.

I have no technical advice or counsel to offer those of you who labor in this vineyard that produces words and pictures. You will forgive me for not telling you the instruments with which you work are miraculous, that your responsibility is unprecedented, or that your aspirations are frequently frustrated. It is not necessary to remind you that the fact that your voice is amplified to the degree where it reaches from one end of the country to the other does not confer upon you greater wisdom or understanding than you possessed when your voice reached only from one end of the bar to the other. . . .

. . . Believing that potentially the commercial system of broadcasting as practiced in this country is the best and freest yet devised, I have decided to express my concern about what I believe to be happening to radio and television. These instruments have been good to me beyond my due. There exists in my mind no reasonable grounds for personal complaint. I have no feud, either with my employers, any sponsors, or with the professional critics of radio and television. But I am seized with an abiding fear regarding what these two instruments are doing to our society, our culture, and our heritage. . . .

Our history will be what we make it. And if there are any historians about fifty or a hundred years from now, and there should be preserved the kinescopes for one week of all three networks, they will there find recorded in black-and-white, or color, evidence of decadence, escapism, and insulation from the realities of the world in which we live. I invite your attention to the television schedules of all three networks between the hours of 8 and 11 P.M., Eastern Time. Here you will find only fleeting and spasmodic reference to the fact that this nation is in mortal danger. There are, it is true, occasional informative programs presented in that intellectual ghetto on Sunday afternoons. But during the daily peak viewing period, television in the main insulates us from the world in which we live. If this state of affairs continues, we may alter an advertising slogan to read: Look Now, Pay Later. For surely we shall pay for using this most powerful instrument of communication to insulate the citizenry from the hard and demanding realities which must be faced if we are to survive. I mean the word "survive" literally. If there were to be a competition in indifference, or perhaps in insulation from reality, then Nero and his fiddle, Chamberlain and his umbrella, could not find a place on an early afternoon sustaining show. If Hollywood were to run out of Indians, the program schedules would be mangled beyond all recognition. Then some courageous soul with a small budget might be able to do a documentary telling what, in fact, we have done — and are still doing — to the Indians in this country. But that would be unpleasant. And we must at all costs shield the sensitive citizens from anything that is unpleasant. . . .

I am entirely persuaded that the American public is more reasonable, restrained, and more mature than most of our industry's program planners believe. Their fear of controversy is not warranted by the evidence. I have reason to know, as do many of you, that when the evidence on a controversial subject is fairly and calmly presented, the public recognizes it for what it is — an effort to illuminate rather than to agitate. . . .

. . . The oldest excuse of the networks for their timidity is their youth. Their spokesmen say, "We are young; we have not developed the traditions nor acquired the experience of the older media." If they but knew it, they are building those traditions, creating those precedents every day. Each time they yield to a voice from Washington or any political pressure, each time they eliminate something that might offend some section of the community, they are creating their own body of precedent and tradition. . . .

. . . The top management of the networks, with a few notable exceptions, has been trained in advertising, research, sales, or show business. But by the nature of the corporate structure, they also make the final and crucial decisions having to do with news and public affairs. Frequently they have neither the time nor the competence to do this. . . .

. . . I have said . . . that we have in this country a free enterprise system of radio and television which is superior to any other. But to achieve its promise, it must be both free and enterprising. There is no suggestion here that networks or individual stations should operate as philanthropies. But I can find nothing in the Bill of Rights or the Communications Act which says they must increase their profits each year, lest the Republic collapse.

. . . Every licensee who applies for a grant to operate in the public interest, convenience, and necessity makes certain promises about what he will do in terms of program content. Many recipients of licenses have, in blunt language, welshed on those promises. The moneymaking machine somehow blunts their memories. . . .

. . . I am frightened by the imbalance, the constant striving to reach the largest possible audience for everything; by the absence of a sustained study of the state of the nation. Heywood Broun once said, "No body politic is healthy until it begins to itch." I would like television to produce some itching pills rather than this endless outpouring of tranquilizers. . . .

. . . Why should not each of the twenty or thirty big corporations which dominate radio and television decide that they should give up one or two of their regularly scheduled programs each year, turn the time over to the networks, and say in effect, "This is a tiny tithe, just a little of our profits. On this particular night, we aren't going to try to sell cigarettes or automobiles; this is merely a gesture to indicate our belief in the importance of ideas." . . . I would reckon that the president, and indeed the stockholders of the corporation who sponsored such a venture, would feel just a little bit better about the corporation and the country.

. . . Unless we get up off our fat surpluses and recognize that television in the main is being used to distract, delude, amuse, and insulate us, then television and those who finance it, those who look at it, and those who work at it, may see a totally different picture too late. . . .

I do not advocate that we turn television into a twenty-seven-inch wailing wall, where longhairs constantly moan about the state of our culture and our defense. But I would just like to see it reflect occasionally the hard, unyielding realities of the world in which we live. . . .

. . . This instrument can teach, it can illuminate; yes, it can even inspire. But it can do so only to the extent that humans are determined to use it to those ends. Otherwise it is merely wires and lights in a box. There is a great and perhaps decisive battle to be fought against ignorance, intolerance, and indifference. This weapon of television could be useful. . . .

Stonewall Jackson . . . said, "When war comes, you must draw the sword and throw away the scabbard." The problem with television is that it is rusting in the scabbard during a battle for survival.

Ed Murrow knew exactly what he was doing in that Chicago speech. He was acting from his personal hurt but also from the frustration that a great resource was being squandered. Ed's foundation had been in education, and television wasn't educating. He fully intended to vent his anger and awaken the industry, but he also hoped that television would address his idea for prime time public affairs programs. There certainly was an element of bridge-burning in the speech, but Ed had a lot of insulation. NBC repeatedly told him he could jump to that network at any salary he desired. He also had options outside of broadcasting.

It's possible that Ed believed he had nothing to lose professionally or otherwise because he was a very sick man at the close of 1958. His colleagues saw him grow weaker. Writer Ed Bliss, who worked with him every day, believed Murrow was already dying. On election night, relegated to covering regional returns from a studio catwalk, Murrow spent hours on his feet and was exhausted by the close of the broadcast at two in the morning.

At year's end, Murrow, physically and emotionally drained, was behaving erratically, snapping at dinner party guests, and sometimes disappearing for a day or two. He told friends that he was managing only an hour or two of sleep each night. One night in January, minutes before his nightly radio broadcast, Murrow handed his script to Blair Clark and asked him to do the program. Bliss then saw Murrow, standing at some file cabinets, put his head down on his folded arms and cry. A medical exam had revealed a bronchospasm, and the doctor feared he might have pulmonary emphysema. In February 1959 Ed decided to take a year's leave of absence, to begin in July.

TV critics viewed the sabbatical announcement as Ed's concession of defeat in a power struggle with his employer. CBS saw it as another piece of bad publicity following the cancellation of *See It Now*, Murrow's speech in Chicago, and prosecutors looking into the quiz shows. Now the network's journalistic legend wanted to be away. Executives held meetings to develop some sort of image enhancer. In May, CBS president Frank Stanton announced that there would be a new prime time news program in the fall.

Ed's plan to take time off was a godsend for Sig Mickelson. He was in charge of news at CBS, but he had never been in charge of Murrow and Friendly. The *See It Now* unit acted on its own and took its problems directly to board chairman Bill Paley. The new public affairs program would be launched in Murrow's absence, so it would be a Friendly-only production. Friendly pleaded with Mickelson to keep the team together. In the end, Mickelson agreed only that Murrow could appear on some of the programs but would not co-produce and would not be the principal reporter. Murrow was disappointed that Friendly ultimately agreed to take the job on those terms.

Before leaving on a world trip with his wife and son, Ed Murrow closed two chapters in his career. On Friday, June 26, 1959, he did his last nightly radio broadcast, ending a program that had run continuously since he left his executive job in 1947. That same night he hosted *Person to Person* for the last time. Charles Collingwood would have the show from then on. The broadcasting life of Edward R. Murrow now consisted entirely of *Small World*, which he continued to host while on sabbatical.

Ed, Janet, and Casey Murrow left for Sweden in August, with the family's Ford Thunderbird in the hold of the ship. What should have been a nice year of relaxation for a sick fifty-one-year-old man was nothing of the sort. Reporters met the ship at the dock. Then there were receptions, meetings, and appointments to keep in Stockholm, Oslo, and Copenhagen. While in Denmark, Ed learned he was to travel to Teheran to interview the shah of Iran for CBS. Janet enrolled Casey in a boarding school in Switzerland and was reunited with Ed in London. That's when the bottom really dropped out of their so-called sabbatical.

Back home, the quiz show investigation was now the quiz show scandal. Fourteen former contestants were arrested and charged with perjury. Television networks, although not directly implicated in the scandal, were blamed for running a massive scam, and critics hammered TV for its greed and corruption. In October, Frank Stanton addressed the convention of the Radio-Television News Directors Association, the very forum at which Ed had torched the broadcasting industry a year earlier. Stanton promised that hereafter CBS would be honest with its viewers and not be party to anything that was not what it purported to be. Jack Gould of the *New York Times* followed up with Stanton. What did the CBS president mean? Stanton told him the network would do away with canned applause and laugh tracks on its shows and, he added, it would tell viewers that certain interview programs included questions and answers that had been rehearsed. Gould asked if Stanton was referring to *Person to Person*. Stanton said yes.

It was not a slip of the tongue, and Stanton never claimed it was. He had gratuitously and probably deliberately linked the most beloved figure in broadcast journalism with the worst scandal in the history of the broadcasting industry. It was revenge, not just for Murrow's RTNDA speech, but also for all the times Murrow had ignored Stanton's directives and had taken his concerns directly to Bill Paley. There was a chain of command, and Murrow had violated it by tapping his long-standing friendship with the company's founder. That very friendship had clouded Murrow's vision. He refused to acknowledge that Stanton was Paley's hatchet man, doing the dirty work that had to be done in the running of a big conglomerate such as CBS. Murrow could not blame his old friend Paley for the heartless corporate giant CBS had become. It had to be Stanton. So Stanton became for Murrow the symbol of everything that had gone wrong since those halcyon days of triumph following the war. Stanton was the bogeyman.

Ed did not respond for several days. He was busy preparing for two British broadcasts and a speech. He waited for CBS to issue a correction, a press release clearing up any confusion in the network president's remarks, a statement that Stanton had misspoken. There was no such statement. Ed's reply to Stanton appeared in the *New York Times* on Sunday, October 25:

Dr. Frank Stanton has finally revealed

his ignorance of both news and the requirements of production. . . . He suggests that *Person to Person* . . . was not what it purported to be. . . . I am sorry Dr. Stanton believes that I have participated in perpetrating a fraud on the public. My conscience is clear. His seems to be bothering him.

A lawyer was dispatched to London to obtain a written apology from Murrow. Ralph Colin arrived on Tuesday, the Murrows' silver wedding anniversary. Instead of their planned drive through the English countryside, the Murrows listened to Colin try to fashion some language acceptable to Ed. Colin left with a statement that sounded more like a Stanton apology. Ed probably would have been fired if the quiz show scandal hadn't been so much in the news. CBS wanted no more bad publicity. Yet Murrow's status with CBS was left unresolved and hung over his head for the rest of the sabbatical. He tried several times, unsuccessfully, to determine if he'd been fired.

Ed and Janet reclaimed Casey from boarding school and drove the T-bird across Europe. Janet took ill, then Ed, and none of them felt well as the trip continued to Israel and India. After stops in Thailand, Cambodia, Hong Kong, Honolulu and a visit with the family in Washington, the sabbatical was over — months early. Ed was back in New York by late May 1960.

News at CBS had changed dramatically in his absence. Producers were dominant now, not reporters. Ed was now a reporter who worked for producer Fred Friendly. Middle managers had orders to read Ed's copy and tell superiors when it might contain something to which the bosses would object. In the new CBS, Ed Murrow never quite fit. In addition, *Small World* was canceled; its sponsor transferred to the new public affairs series *CBS Reports*.

In July Ed started a new radio program, this time on a once-a-week basis. *Background*, produced by Ed Bliss, also made use of the still very formidable roster of CBS correspondents around the world.

Murrow worked the 1960 political conventions as a floor reporter until Don Hewitt suggested that Ed join Walter Cronkite at the CBS convention anchor desk. Hewitt was hopeful for something that would counter NBC's popular anchor duo of Chet Huntley and David Brinkley. Hewitt's long career included lots of great ideas, but he counted this one as his worst. Cronkite resented having to share the role with Murrow, while Murrow understood he was just being used for window dressing. It might have signified the passing of Murrow's time and the dawning of Cronkite's, but the two great titans of CBS News shared no chemistry, and it showed.

There was one project in which Ed found great satisfaction. "Harvest of Shame" was not a Murrow/Friendly production, but Ed threw himself into putting the documentary together. Produced by David Lowe and filmed by Marty Barnett, "Harvest of Shame" concerned the conditions endured by migrant laborers, the people with whom Ed had worked in the fields and sawmills of Washington many years earlier. The program specifically dealt with farm workers in Florida, and Ed went there several times to see their situation firsthand. He was deeply involved in the writing and made suggestions for the film editing. It was not his program, but it bears his mark.

In the fall, Ed's lungs gave out again and he suffered his worst pulmonary attacks in twenty years. Pneumonia sidelined him for election night. He hated missing the story, but he didn't care much for either candidate. He still blamed Nixon for Laurence Duggan's death, and Kennedy carried the double baggage of having a father who had wanted to appease Hitler and a brother who had worked for McCarthy's legal team.

"Harvest of Shame" was broadcast on the day after Thanksgiving. Viewers, having enjoyed their holiday bounty, learned about the people who put all that food on their tables. Growers were outraged at being pictured as exploiters of rural blacks, poor whites, and illegal immigrants, perhaps giving Paley his last Murrow-induced stomachache. "Harvest of Shame" may have provided enough background to contribute to the later successes of Cesar Chavez and the United Farm Workers, but its legacy is curious. "Harvest of Shame" is still regarded as one of the classic TV documentaries, yet updates in subsequent decades by NBC and PBS showed the scene pretty much as Lowe, Barnett, and Murrow had seen it. It was still hard, backbreaking stoop work in the hot sun performed by the nation's most vulnerable population of workers.

The program was a final triumph for Murrow at CBS. He knew his position there was untenable. On January 22, 1961,

Edward R. Murrow did his final CBS radio broadcast, in which he commented on the outgoing and incoming presidents. Before the week was over, he accepted President Kennedy's offer to become director of the United States Information Agency. A quarter century with CBS was over. He would no longer be a "problem" for the network whose quality and credibility he'd done so much to establish. Likewise, CBS would no longer be a problem for him.

10

USIA

Despite the ugliness of his relationship with CBS at the end, Murrow, as he began government service, still sought advice from the CBS chairman. Bill Paley told him he should insist on access to JFK's inner circle and be included in all meetings of the cabinet and the National Security Council. Ed told Paley that Kennedy had given him those assurances. Yet in April 1961, when Cubans trained by the CIA landed at the Bay of Pigs, he didn't hear about it at any Kennedy administration meeting, but instead got it secondhand from a reporter at the *New York Times.* Ed protested both the policy ("a stupid idea") and his exclusion from important discussions.

After that fiasco, Ed was, in fact, present for cabinet and NSC meetings. JFK liked Ed's advice to delay resumption of nuclear testing despite the Soviet Union's resumption of tests. The president remarked that he wished he'd had Murrow's counsel on Cuba.

The mission of the United States Information Agency is "to tell America's story abroad," although it's always the government's version of that story and told as a means of backing foreign policy goals. Ed's journalistic itch to tell the truth clashed with his new government official's fear that the truth could be used to smear America's image. No sooner was he named to his new post than he was trying to stop the BBC from broadcasting "Harvest of Shame," his last major TV program for CBS. Jack Gould of the *New York Times*, so much a fan of the CBS Murrow, urged the USIA Murrow to resign. The BBC declined to stop the broadcast, and Ed dropped the matter.

Another conflict between the public Murrow and the private Murrow concerned the Telstar satellite, a technological breakthrough that launched the modern world of communications — broadcast and otherwise. Telstar was developed for the government, but the government decided to turn it over to industry. Ed was outraged at such a corporate giveaway; the people had paid for it, and it should be used for their benefit. His duty, however, required him to testify in Congress on behalf of the bill authorizing the transfer of Telstar to commercial interests. He acknowledged his awkwardness under questioning by Senator Albert Gore Sr.

Ed's requests for agency budget increases reflected his agreement with Kennedy administration goals to reach out to Latin America and Africa. Getting those additional funds meant doing something else out of character for a journalist — making nice with Congress. Ed's lobbying was one of his principal failures as a bureaucrat. Failing to win a budget boost, he compounded the problem by making speeches blasting the very people he was asking for money. That's just not how it's done in Washington.

Although now in government, Ed did not abandon efforts to make television better. He was among those dissatisfied with the sameness and the limited offerings of the three networks. The Ford Foundation and the Carnegie Corporation were interested in providing seed money for a fourth network. Ed wrote a proposal for Ford in which he suggested staffing the new venture with quality newspeople who were still at the commercial networks because they lacked an alternative. He envisioned the fourth network as one that would shame the established commercial networks with the quality of its programs and become the conscience of broadcasting. He pointedly said the new network should not be handicapped by any association with the word "education." Ed was offered the job of programming news for the new network, with a guarantee of complete freedom to do as he pleased. He decided he had not been in government long enough to give up on public service. These early notions of Murrow and others were the brainstorming that resulted in the Public Broadcasting Service, a network that does not have the word "education" in its name.

Ed was sick again on a trip to Europe in the fall of 1962, but continued on to Teheran, where he was hospitalized. U.S. Army doctors diagnosed pleurisy. Returning home, he entered Bethesda Naval Hospital, where doctors dismissed a spot on his lung as likely an old scar from past lung problems. The month he was away from the office was a critical period in the JFK presidency. Ed had missed the entire Cuban missile crisis.

Vietnam concerned the Kennedy administration in 1963 because a decision had to be made on whether to increase involvement. It was a crucial point in a matter that would consume the country through 1975 and have fallout that would last much longer. Ed Murrow was drawn into it because the USIA was assigned to convince reporters in Saigon that the government of Ngo Dinh Diem embodied the hopes and dreams of the Vietnamese people. Ed knew the Diem government did no such thing because he had identified which government advisers were giving JFK the best counsel. He was especially drawn to the frank reports of Roger Hilsman, the State Department's research and intelligence man. Ed also was reading the dispatches of the young correspondents for the *New York Times* who had figured out that the corrupt Diem government was a loser. The USIA director was absorbing the reporting of journalists who were laughing at the efforts of his agency.

Ed supported increasing the number of advisers to sixteen thousand as a middle ground between abandoning the Saigon government or backing the hawks who wanted a hundred thousand or more U.S. troops deployed. He opposed the Agent Orange defoliation program.

For decades we have pondered whether

our Vietnam disaster might have been avoided had President Kennedy not been assassinated. We might also ask whether it might have been avoided had Edward R. Murrow been around to advise Kennedy's successor.

In September 1963 Ed Murrow entered Washington Hospital Center, where doctors discovered that same spot on his left lung that Bethesda Naval doctors had dismissed a year earlier. Ed had cancer, and the doctors removed the lung. The good news was that the man who'd smoked sixty-five cigarettes a day for decades was now a nonsmoker. The bad news was that the cancer wasn't gone.

He was still at home recovering when President Kennedy was assassinated in Dallas. He exhausted himself climbing stairs to the East Room at the White House to pay his last respects.

Like others in the Kennedy administration, Ed submitted his resignation when JFK was killed. He officially left government in mid-January 1964, after three years of service.

Dr. Jonas Salk took a personal interest in Ed's recovery and found the Murrows a place in La Jolla, California. Bill Paley visited Ed in La Jolla, and the two restored their old friendship. Paley was heartened that Ed seemed so interested in what was going on at CBS.

Morale at CBS, very low when Murrow left, had grown even worse. Late in 1961, Howard K. Smith had been fired over a documentary that was supposed to be Ed's. "Who Speaks for Birmingham?" was a *CBS Reports* program that was broadcast after Freedom Riders were brutally beaten by the Ku Klux Klan. Smith had witnessed the attack and wanted to end the program quoting Edmund Burke: "The only thing necessary for the triumph of evil is for good men to do nothing." The quote was not allowed, and Smith left CBS after a shouting match with Paley. Both Smith and Bill Downs would end their careers reporting for ABC News. Another Murrow Boy departed in 1962 when Larry LeSueur joined the Voice of America.

In 1962, network news shifted its focus to the nightly newscast. Douglas Edwards, TV's first network anchorman, was replaced on *The CBS Evening News*, the program he'd been doing since 1948. Edwards became CBS Radio's principal anchorman and had a midday newscast on TV. His replacement on *The CBS Evening News* was

Walter Cronkite, and the broadcast was expanded to thirty minutes on Labor Day 1963. The program had a Murrow presence of sorts with Eric Sevareid providing analysis, and Murrow's radio writer Ed Bliss serving as editor.

Fred Friendly became president of CBS News in 1964, but his old partner did not cheer the news. Murrow regarded Friendly as a great producer who was out of place as an executive. One of Friendly's first acts was to rehire Joe Wershba, who had left CBS in the blacklisting days. Friendly would leave CBS just two years later, when the network insisted on showing its usual daytime programs instead of the Fulbright hearings on Vietnam.

By May 1964 the Murrows had returned to New York. Ed felt better and talked of going back to work, possibly making documentaries for public television, yet he was not up to delivering the commencement address at Casey's graduation from Milton Academy.

In late summer, Tess and Bill Shirer were invited to the Murrows' Glen Arden Farm in Pawling, New York. Ed wanted to patch things up with the original Murrow Boy, the man with whom he shared his first CBS broadcast in 1938. Several times Ed tried to bring up their differences from 1947, but Shirer cut him off. Shirer would not absolve the man he blamed for destroying his broadcasting career, even though the man was dying. Just months before his own death in 1993, Shirer was still expressing his bitterness toward Murrow, yet also his fondness for the man.

In September 1964 Ed was awarded the Presidential Medal of Freedom, America's highest peacetime civilian honor. An awards event the following month in New York was his last public appearance.

Doctors at New York Hospital removed a tumor near his brain in November. Discharged on Christmas Day, he remained in the city and was visited by friends. Most knew they were seeing him for the last time.

He was back in the hospital in March, just as he received word that Queen Elizabeth was making him a knight commander of the British Empire. Two weeks later, he begged to go home to the farm.

On April 25, 1965, Edward R. Murrow turned fifty-seven years old. Two days later, he died. His ashes were scattered at his country home, Glen Arden Farm, in Pawling, New York.

Afterword

On the day Ed Murrow died, Eric Sevareid eulogized his old friend and colleague on *The CBS Evening News.* Sevareid said of Murrow, "He was a shooting star and we shall not see his like again." It was both a tribute and a safe prediction.

The founder only passes by once. Murrow's accomplishments can't be duplicated because he was writing on a blank page. On a single day in 1938 he pioneered the overseas network reporting staff and the roundup news format while reinventing himself, transforming a junior executive into a foreign correspondent. Then in 1951, he moved television beyond its function as a headline service and established it as an original news source, not a medium that merely duplicated stories culled from newspapers. He also gave broadcast journalism a set of standards that matched those of the best newspapers in terms of what stories to cover and how to cover them. From two platforms of show business he carved out space for serious investigation and discussion of public affairs. Although he knew how to entertain, as shown by the success of *Person to Person*, he was adamant about keeping entertainment out of broadcast journalism.

If Sevareid meant we would not see the like of Murrow the individual, his prediction still holds. We all know people who possess one or more of Murrow's qualities, but no one has them all to the degree he did. He was the embodiment of the American Dream. Born among the hardscrabble dirt farmers of Polecat Creek, North Carolina, and raised among the migrant laborers and lumberjacks of rural Washington, he never lost his working-class values. Although comfortable in the company of janitors and diplomats, he could also be shy and awkward, sometimes even with close associates. Unable to make small talk and unwilling to fake it, he felt no guilt about subjecting people to long silences. He knew a wide range of remarkable people, gave away a great deal of money, and found jobs for dozens of acquaintances, yet believed he had no real friends.

Murrow was a good manager, leading by example rather than by meetings and memos, and he was a near-flawless judge of talent. He was smart but not brilliant, his mind working skillfully like the debater he was in college. His scripts presented his case in an orderly, lawyerlike manner. Education was his first profession and he truly was a teacher, ever anxious to learn something new and to pass it on in what he called the biggest classroom in the world. He had a moral code rooted in populism and justice, taking the side of the underdog and taking the starch out of the stuffed shirts.

Most of all, Murrow was absolutely fearless. His favorite commentator, Elmer Davis, used to say, "Don't let the bastards scare you." Nothing scared Murrow — not bombs, dictators, generals, members of Congress, sponsors, corporate executives, or Joseph McCarthy. Murrow could not be muscled, bullied, bought, corrupted, or intimidated. He could, however, be flawed in judgment, as he was with Frank Stanton. It was convenient for Murrow to see Stanton as the enemy of news. Six years after Murrow's death, Stanton risked a prison sentence for contempt by refusing to give a congressional committee outtakes from a CBS *Reports* documentary called "The Selling of the Pentagon." Even Murrow would have had to concede that Stanton was a champion of journalism that day.

The real reason we'll not see Murrow's like again is that everything that allowed Murrow to be Murrow has changed dramatically. Murrow benefited from being the standard to whom all who follow should be compared. When you're the "first" at something you get to write a lot of your own rules.

When Murrow came home from Europe after World War II, he enjoyed enormous goodwill on at least two continents. He was much more than a radio star or even a vastly respected journalist; he also was a man who had served his country in a new and distinctive way. From the annexation of Austria in 1938 to the liberation of Buchenwald in 1945 — and beyond, Murrow had put World War II into the living rooms of America in a manner that newspapers, for all their virtues, could not. He had endeared himself and CBS to all who had been through so much for so long. As a result, he possessed a stock of goodwill that he used to hire an all-star staff of reporters and produce innovative and exciting programs with the full endorsement of CBS management. For years after leaving his executive position and returning to daily reporting, he continued to use the capital he'd acquired from his war reporting. It gave him insulation from network executives who were supposed to be his superiors. There was a standard for Murrow and a different set of standards for everyone else. Such a circumstance likely will never prevail again. It is unique to that time, that man, and that situation.

Murrow's relationship with CBS founder William Paley is another one-of-a-kind circumstance. Since today's networks are commercial properties of huge conglomerates, a contemporary Murrow/Paley relationship couldn't happen even if an anchorman married the CEO's daughter. The bond between Murrow and Paley was forged in wartime London, where the young correspondent was host to his network's chairman. The tycoon was Colonel Paley then, advising Eisenhower on the use of radio in psychological warfare. Murrow and Paley walked the streets together as the bombs fell. They shared their dreams of what CBS could be. Murrow made sure his boss met all the right people in government, the military, and high society. They were from radically different backgrounds and circumstances, yet both were extraordinary men of action who recognized the brains, gifts, and talents in each other. Many postwar reorganizations of CBS put various layers of management between Paley and Murrow, yet both men ignored them. Murrow believed he worked for Paley and no one else, so he took his problems directly to the chairman. Everyone at CBS knew of Murrow's pipeline to Paley and backed off from supervision, much less criticism, of the founder's buddy. The relationship served Murrow and all associated with him until the last few years of Murrow's tenure at CBS, when Paley began to regard Murrow's aggressive journalism as a liability to network business interests. In the end, Murrow learned he was just a hired hand on Mr. Paley's farm; Murrow's independence of the corporate structure vanished. As the journalist A. J. Leibling said: "Freedom of the press is guaranteed only to those who own one." Paley owned one and Murrow did not.

Viewers in Murrow's day had no remote, nor did they need one. Surfing was still done at the beach in the 1950s. Viewers had three choices, and many had only two, because a lot of ABC stations were UHF, requiring additional equipment. We watched what Dad wanted to see, and that could be wrestling and

Roller Derby or it could be *Playhouse 90*, depending on Dad's measure of evolution. Cable TV was still in development. Murrow didn't have to compete with a hundred or more channels; he just had to beat NBC. If *See It Now* were to pop up today on PBS or the Discovery Channel, would anyone notice?

Politics has changed radically since the days of Murrow, when the left wing did not control the Democratic Party and the right wing did not control the Republican Party. Many of today's public affairs programs reflect the polarized political climate and are overtly partisan to entertain listeners and viewers whose minds are already made up. People no longer tune in to a program for a detached assessment of political matters; they tune in to have their own biases affirmed. A Murrow program inviting an audience to think might not fare well today.

The principal reason why we are not likely to see a Murrow again is that Murrow was bad for business. Yes, he attracted listeners and viewers to CBS, consistently won the industry's top awards, was widely praised by critics in the newspapers, and gave CBS some class within a program schedule designed to appeal to the lowest common denominator. Those assets, however, were not sufficient to cure Bill Paley of his stomachaches. CBS management regarded *See It Now* as a ratings loser that angered politicians, vexed sponsors, and alienated southern affiliate stations when it carried programs on civil rights. The program might have been killed sooner except that CBS in those days still had a commitment to public service, a notion almost quaint today. Murrow invoked that commitment when he fought for his programs, arguing that CBS should be broadcasting serious journalism because it was the right thing to do. It mattered not to Murrow that the news division was a tiny component of a diversified corporation involved in enterprises in and out of broadcasting. Paley was trying to make money, not save the world; Murrow believed CBS could do both.

Murrow never had to put up with corporate bean counters to the degree that today's broadcast journalists must endure. In Murrow's time, news was a loss leader and wasn't expected to score big ratings and make money. That changed dramatically in the 1980s when the networks were acquired by huge firms that dwarfed the Paley-size corporations. Public service was a luxury the new media conglomerates could not afford. With network audiences dwindling because of the wider availability of cable TV, the news divisions now were expected to top the competition in the ratings and to make money. From public service to profit center is a jolting transition, but it happened. It began with deep cuts in expenses, which were fine as long as they involved trading limos for vans and first-class airfare for coach, but then it involved people. Hundreds of fine journalists lost their jobs in the 1980s when the networks pared back. When the bloodletting was over, the quest for profit took a different direction.

The networks decided that the way to attract an audience to news programming was to change the look and the definition of news. The model for the transformation already existed at each network's affiliated stations where local newscasts were informal presentations heavy on eye-catching features, crime, and celebrity gossip while light on politics and policy.

If there is a moment in broadcast history at which the legacy of Edward R. Murrow died, it is probably March 6, 1981, when Walter Cronkite did his last broadcast for *The CBS Evening News*. Though Murrow and Cronkite were not close, they shared certain values about the importance of public affairs and how news should be presented. A Cronkite program opened with sounds of newsroom ambience — distant muffled voices and the clatter of wire service teletype machines in those precomputer days. Viewers were given a billboard advising that Dan Rather would be reporting from the White House, Roger Mudd from Capitol Hill, Marvin Kalb from the State Department, Peter Kalischer and Bert Quint from capitals overseas, Daniel Schorr from some Washington agency or another, analysis by Eric Sevareid, and perhaps, as the cherry on the sundae, Charles Kuralt *On the Road*, the only element of a Cronkite program that might count as "light" fare. "Visuals" consisted of tasteful slides of maps, drawings, or photographs made to appear electronically over Cronkite's shoulder. Judging from the look of *The CBS Evening News* after he retired, one got the impression that Cronkite's bosses were glad to see him go. Theme music opened the program and graphics shot up, down, and around Dan Rather from every direction, in some cases spinning and tumbling into view. Later, sound effects were added, boosting the graphics through their trajectory to make sure we'd notice that some visual spice was part of the mix. As for content, you'd have thought Washington, D.C., had shut down. Gone were many of the stories that alerted viewers to the daily status of our democratic republic. The changes reflected new leadership at the top of CBS News, who wanted a more contemporary look on the screen and content that appealed to the pulse, not the mind. The new CBS News wanted "moments," stories that played on viewers' emotions, and "back fence" stories, something light that neighbors might mention to one another over the back fence.

Walter Cronkite, "the most trusted man in America," led CBS out of the depths of low morale following Murrow's departure, reestablished his network as number one in the ratings, and kept it there until he retired, but his employer of thirty years found him boring. The Cronkite meat and potatoes diet of Washington and foreign news didn't appeal to CBS in the 1980s which fancied the nouvelle cuisine of "moments." Imagine what the bored CBS managers would have thought of Murrow, who, in his 1958 RTNDA speech, argued for the occasional prime-time program on the state of American education, U.S. policy in the Middle East, and the status of NATO. This is not exactly back fence material. Murrow also urged programming that would "exalt the importance of ideas and information"; those provided "moments" for him.

It's difficult to imagine Murrow lasting very long in broadcast journalism today because his programs would be required to make money. Nonbroadcasters acquired the networks in the 1980s when the FCC no longer mandated public service programming. The new owners, principally concerned with profits and share prices, ordered the network news divisions to be profitable. They saw no reason why the news division should not be a profit center, just like the movie studio, publishing house, or other properties they owned. When news has to make money, the substance, character, and look of the news changes. In the public service era, the networks produced documentaries. In the profit era, documentaries have been replaced by magazine programs heavy on crime, items about celebrities, feel-good features, and the latest trendy disease. These programs have to compete with entertainment programs in prime time. The only way a news program can compete in prime time is to become an entertainment program.

Ironically, the best and most successful of the magazine programs is the one that most closely follows the traditional definition of news. In 1968, when Don Hewitt developed *60 Minutes* for CBS, he set out to combine elements of "high Murrow" (*See It Now*) and "low Murrow" (*Person to Person*). Murrow might be happy on *60 Minutes* until the first time the CBS lawyers told him there was something he couldn't say.

Cable TV might seem like a good platform for Murrow, offering lots of airtime for lots of news. Cable relieved the broadcast networks of the pressure to provide live coverage of important breaking stories. Cable claims to have all-news channels, and indeed it does when there is important breaking news. In fact, when an important story breaks, the so-called all-news channels cover *only* that one story, upsetting those who feel "all news" should provide "all of the news." It's obsessive total coverage, whether it's a legitimate story on war in Iraq, or a celebrity story like the death of JFK Jr., which ran for nearly a week. On most days, however, cable TV offers no news in prime time (except on the headline channel) because news simply can't compete with prime-time entertainment programs. It's a sad fact that cable TV, with plenty of airtime available to explore important, complex issues in great detail, squanders that resource by descending to tabloid sensationalism, personality cult shows, and aping talk radio with high-testosterone shout shows requiring panelists and viewers alike to wake up angry and stay angry. What would Murrow say about the cable news anchor who interviewed a psychic regarding the disappearance of a Washington intern who was having an affair with a congressman? How could Murrow do a program on education if his cable bosses insisted he talk with "experts" about the woman who killed her husband by driving the family car over his cheating carcass three times? Murder is committed every day in the United States, and although it is unacceptable in every case, the clutter of crime news distracts us from matters we can do something about. We should concern ourselves with issues that affect our common welfare, not some tawdry episode that has nothing to instruct us on how to get through a day. For ratings' sake, cable news focuses too often on the titillating and not on the news we really need.

That leaves public broadcasting, which is sometimes balanced to a fault. A liberal writer once joked that he expected Jim Lehrer to say, "Here with a different view of Hitler is . . ." Murrow believed it was wrong to recruit a liar to be part of a program in order to balance the truth. Murrow's style was a bit too bold for public broadcasting, whose executives have to face government scrutiny. Congress is in the picture because a minuscule amount of government dollars is part of public broadcasting's financing, prompting political partisans and commercial broadcasters to complain that controversial programs are funded by taxpayers. Bill Moyers ends his PBS program *Now* with a commentary. That he does so is considered audacious by those who want public broadcasting to be as bland as an actuarial table.

Murrow could not function in today's journalism. He would be outraged by consultants of the type who told clients that coverage of anti-Iraq war protests was a ratings loser. Murrow, the man who made broadcasting a source of original news, could not abide having news programming determined by market research, nor would he allow focus groups to determine which individuals are worthy of reporting the news. Sadly, those practices are a part of today's TV journalism.

The audience for news programs is an older audience, and one cannot imagine Murrow keeping his temper if lectured by the sales force to do more to reach the eighteen-to-thirty-five-year-old demographic so coveted by advertisers. Likewise, any notion of replacing coverage of public issues with items of gossip or pop culture to appeal to youth, women, or minorities he'd regard as pandering, and an insult to those very groups.

As for radio, which Murrow in his RTNDA speech called "that most satisfying and rewarding instrument," it would neither satisfy nor reward him today. In the 1980s, when radio was relieved of its public service responsibilities, the first casualties were the news departments of the nation's radio stations. Most cities only have one or two stations employing local reporters. Some stations carry headlines provided by services employing people who use different names when reading for multiple stations in the same city. A great many stations don't bother with any news. Commercial radio, on both the local and national levels, has abandoned news and allowed public radio to fill the vacuum.

There are ten thousand radio stations in the United States. As a result of government deregulation, a single company, Clear Channel Communications, owns more than 10 percent of those stations and reaps more than 20 percent of the total industry revenue. Although many of the stations purchased by his company once enjoyed a reputation for quality news coverage, the founder of Clear Channel, Lowry Mays, has other priorities. "We're not in the business of providing news and information," Mays told *Fortune* magazine, "we're simply in the business of selling our customers products." Since its sign-on in 1922, station WHAS in Louisville has been the leading broadcast institution in all of Kentucky. It would take a good-sized warehouse to contain all its awards for distinction in broadcast journalism. Today, however, WHAS is owned by Clear Channel, whose founder declares his firm is "not in the business of providing news and information." One cannot imagine Edward R. Murrow being welcome today at that station, which carried his broadcasts to millions in the eastern United States, including the author of this book.

If there's a Murrow now among young

journalists, he or she will probably leave the business before arriving at a position that gets our attention. If that person shares Murrow's background and training, he or she likely will end up as the president of a small college, enjoy the work, and know the names of every freshman's parents. That would be a very good thing and we should not necessarily mourn the loss of such an individual on a bigger stage.

The fact is that we had Murrow when we needed him most — at the beginning of broadcast journalism, before there was a corrupting requirement that news make money. The profession looks so bad today, in part, because Murrow set the standard so high at its birth. We see a bit of his legacy every time there is an important story and broadcast journalism functions as it's supposed to. It's important to remember that once upon a time we turned to radio and television to entertain us and nothing more. If we expect the broadcast media to inform us, educate us, and enlighten us, it's because Edward R. Murrow led us to believe that they would.

Bibliography

Beblen, Ann Denton. "Mary Marvin Breckinridge Patterson." Thesis submitted to Harvard University, 1982.

Bliss, Edward Jr. *Now the News.* New York: Columbia University Press, 1991.

———, ed. *In Search of Light: The Broadcasts of Edward R. Murrow.* New York: Alfred A. Knopf, 1967.

Boyer, Peter J. *Who Killed CBS?* New York: Random House, 1988.

Buzenberg, Susan, and Bill Buzenberg, eds. *Salant, CBS, and the Battle for the Soul of Broadcast Journalism: The Memoirs of Richard S. Salant.* Boulder, Colo.: Westview Press, 1999.

Cloud, Stanley, and Lynne Olson. *The Murrow Boys.* New York: Houghton Mifflin, 1996.

Cronkite, Walter. *A Reporter's Life.* New York: Alfred A. Knopf, 1996.

Faulk, John Henry. *Fear on Trial.* New York: Simon & Schuster, 1964.

Friendly, Fred W. *Due to Circumstances beyond Our Control.* New York: Random

House, 1967.

Hewitt, Don. *Tell Me a Story.* New York: Public Affairs, 2001.

Kendrick, Alexander. *Prime Time.* Boston: Little, Brown, 1969.

Murrow, Edward R. *This Is London.* New York: Simon & Schuster, 1941.

Paley, William S. *As It Happened.* Garden City, N.Y.: Doubleday, 1979.

Persico, Joseph E. *Edward R. Murrow: An American Original.* New York: McGraw-Hill, 1988.

Schoenbrum, David. *America Inside Out.* New York: McGraw-Hill, 1984.

Schorr, Daniel. *Staying Tuned.* New York: Pocket Books, 2001.

Sevareid, Eric. *Not So Wild a Dream.* New York: Alfred A. Knopf, 1946.

Shirer, William L. *Berlin Diary.* New York: Alfred A. Knopf, 1941.

———. *A Native's Return: 1945–1988.* Boston: Little, Brown, 1990.

———. *The Nightmare Years: 1930–1940.* Boston: Little, Brown, 1984

Smith, Howard K. *Last Train from Berlin.* New York: Alfred A. Knopf, 1942.

———. *Events Leading Up to My Death.* New York: St. Martin's Press, 1996.

Sperber, A. M. *Murrow: His Life and Times.* New York: Freundlich Books, 1986.

About the Author

Bob Edwards has hosted NPR's *Morning Edition*, the most popular program in all broadcast media, since its premiere in November 1979. In 1999, he and the program received a prestigious Peabody Award for "two hours of daily entertainment expertly helmed by a man who embodies the essence of excellence in radio." Also a recipient of the Corporation for Public Broadcasting's Edward R. Murrow Award, he is the author of *Fridays with Red*, which chronicled his radio friendship with legendary sportscaster Red Barber.